YOU DON'T LOOK ADOPTED
a memoir

D1571794

ISBN: 978-0-692-75564-8

Thank you.

Kitty

HBL

Scooter

Kent Bond

Karen Tomlinson

Antonia Bogdanovich

Katie Peuvrelle

Erin Sugrue Divencenzo

The Noepe Center

Carol and Dan

Janie and Mike

and, with all that I am,

Keats (xxxxxxxxxxxx)

Some of the names have been changed.
This is, after all, a book about adoption.

ONCE UPON A TIME

Most of my life I have felt both real and not real. I have felt real in the sense that I have a social security number and an online presence and a pulse, and I have felt not real in the sense that my birth mother wanted nothing to do with me once I arrived. Since an infant is born with a sense of self not separate from the mother, I believe that part of my brain took a nosedive in the gap between mothers, and part of my brain decided I must not exist, and in some crazy unexplainable way, nothing changed in that part of my brain, even as an adult.

When you are in conflict with yourself it's like you're a car whose gas pedal is also the brake. It's hard to get anywhere.

The deepest conflict, the thing that was doing the most damage to me and how I was living my life was that my story, my story that began, *The day I was born,* caused people—primarily my mother—pain, and so, logically, it was a bad story. And if the story of your origin is bad, that means so are you.

The only way I was going to bring the two parts of myself together, the only way I was going to step fully into my life, was to tell my story. I tried to write it for over thirty years, but, along with having a stable romantic relationship, it was something I seemed incapable of accomplishing.

TERMS

When I refer to my mother and father, I don't say *my adoptive mom and dad*, and when I refer to my birth mother and father I don't say *my real mother and father*. For, I would hope, obvious reasons.

PSYCHO

If you want a Vegas wedding or the chance to file a restraining order, date an adopted person, or—really what I am saying: me. This is how it will go. We'll meet and we'll hug because somehow it's like we already know each other. We will marvel at how comfortable we are with each other throughout dinner. You, in particular will marvel. Other girls hold themselves back more, are less available, perhaps. We will go back to my house or your house and have sex. The best thing will be if we have little in common. Perhaps English is not your first language or you are a Republican or you have addiction issues.

I will fall in love with you and start fantasizing about our life together. I will imagine walking your dog. I will imagine learning to cook the foods your mother cooks. I will think of all the ways I can make your life better. I will be one hundred percent in until I start feeling like I am losing my edges, my sense of who I am, and then, if we didn't get to Vegas in time, the relationship will end very suddenly because I will get furious over something you did: maybe you were late to pick me up or maybe you told me not to talk with my mouth full, and I will tell you exactly what is on my mind with all the bitterness I have stored in my guts, and you will wonder what happened to the funny and sweet person you had met not all that long ago.

If you are the one to break up with me, the story will be different. I will think I am going to die, and I will write long emails and texts telling you about the power of my love and how, in five years, you will realize letting go of me was the biggest mistake of your life as no one will be able to love you as completely or as unconditionally as I can. I will walk around feeling like a bell that someone has hit overly hard. I will cry in the car, during yoga, when I wake up in the morning. I will be swimming in a sea of missing you so profound I won't see any shore.

The problem is that part of my brain likes the ache of longing more than it likes the safety of your company. Being with you after the first few dates starts to feel like seeing a movie I've already seen, and I start looking forward to when you drive off for the night so I can get back to the sweet fall of missing you.

But when you disappear, when you stop answering my texts and my calls the sweetness also disappears and I am a wreck. I loved you more than I had ever loved any man. I was meant to be with you. There is no one else, and there will never be another man as perfect for me as you are. I will barely be able to breathe. It's like I have disappeared and all that's left is this pair of lungs that I'm supposed to fill, and it is a hideous task, painful and slow.

I have felt this so many times I can't even count. Each time it is brand new. Each time I think I may not survive. I know that if I can just convince you to come back, to love me, everything will be okay.

It will feel like my *job* to convince you. It will feel that some higher power told me to do it and, really, even if I don't like you much, I have to keep trying to convince you to love me because the force that has the wheel in my brain is telling me this is an urgent matter.

After two or three weeks pass and the hormones and god knows what else settles, I will look back and wonder where I had gone, why I had thought a man none of my friends would have considered viable dating material was the perfect one for me.

I DON'T GET IT

How I can be so independent and so needy is beyond me. Half the time I feel like I will die of loneliness and the other half I feel like I will die if I am not alone. In other words, I'm always on the wrong side of the street.

PUSH

My water never broke with my daughter the way it does in the movies. I went to go to the bathroom late in the night, and I felt the odd slide of the mucous plug falling out. The bloodied jelly floated in the toilet water and I was like a six year old who was about to drive a car for the first time—totally unprepared, disbelieving. My copy of *What to Expect When Expecting* was on the back of the toilet, so I opened it to read what to do in this situation. The book said that if this happened in the middle of the night not to worry about it and to go back to bed. So I did.

In the morning, I told my husband what had happened and he went and looked at the book. What it actually said was get to the hospital. He had a class to teach in two hours and he was already sweating even though it was early morning in March and Houston had yet to heat up.

He brought me to the hospital, helped me get checked in, kissed me and said, "Do not have that baby until I get back."

I wasn't having contractions. I was just a 199-pound woman who was being told it was time, that the baby was coming, that the reason my water hadn't broken was because her head was, essentially, blocking the drain. I was brought into a delivery room that looked like the Comfort Inn and given a dose of Pitocin to start the contractions. I went from 0-60 in a very short time, and the breathing routines I'd learned in the prenatal classes were useless. I breathed to survive—there was no organization to the inhales and exhales. If I could have gotten out of bed, I would have climbed the walls.

I had imagined that labor and delivery would be like running the mile. The hardest part would be the third lap, and I had imagined I would just have to pace myself and focus on the parts of my body that didn't hurt: my hands, maybe, my feet, but I was not prepared for the entire-body sickness that labor had brought with it. It felt like the worst case of food poisoning imaginable. There was no place for my brain to settle that didn't hurt, so I just breathed the best I could while saying *ow* over and over, waiting for my husband to get back from teaching class.

This was before the days of cell phones, so he hadn't known about the Pitocin, hadn't known I was deep in labor, and he had stopped to get some lunch before heading to the hospital. I thought I was going to die by the time he arrived, and I needed his hand, his words of encouragement, his steady support. Saying no to the epidural had been a dumb idea. I had thought it was important to feel the birth, but the birth I had imagined was less intense.

When Keats started to come out, I knew I would split in half. It was terrifying and made no sense to me, but the doctor and the nurses and my husband were all encouraging me to push, so even though it seemed that was the stupidest idea in the world, I pushed a bowling ball through what felt like a straw. Her head emerged but her shoulders were stuck. "Oh," the doctor said. "Big baby." He made a cut that I didn't feel, and out Keats slid. My husband started to cry and I looked down and I saw her, thick-bodied, black-haired and slick with birth muck.

"You did it," my husband said. "Keats is finally here. Our daughter."

Neither one of us could take our eyes off her. She was already calm, already looking around like a quiet fish, doing that thing she would do for the rest of her childhood: assessing the situation to figure out the best way to respond.

She was the first person I had ever seen who was related to me by blood, and the irony of it was, because her father was Japanese, she looked adopted.

NOT ME

I first talked to my birth mother over the phone when I was in my forties after a search agency turned up her high school picture and current address for me, and when she answered the phone, her response to my introduction was so canned it was like she'd been standing by the phone all those years, waiting for me to call so she could tell me her story.

"You have the wrong person," she said and I listened to her talk about her cousin, how her cousin was my birth mother, how her cousin had gotten drunk and had had sex at a party that she, Beth, my birth mother had given, and so that Beth had felt responsible and had let her cousin use her, Beth's, identity when she gave birth at the hospital. The story continued. Shortly after my birth, Beth said, her cousin, my supposed birth mother, was in a car accident on the George Washington Bridge. "You were adopted by good people," Beth said to me in her flat voice. "This was a closed adoption. I need you to leave me alone."

I didn't know what to say, so I asked if she could write down the story and mail it to me. She reluctantly agreed and I gave her my name and address. I wasn't sure she was actually writing it down, but a week later I got an envelope with my name and address in scratchy handwriting. Both my first name and last name were spelled wrong.

The story she had told me on the phone was repeated in the letter. Years later I would show the letter to her son, my half-brother, and he would tell me that it wasn't her handwriting. We would puzzle over this fact. I didn't tell him, but my name for her since the day on the phone was The Bitch from New Jersey. All I had wanted from her was the truth. I wasn't looking for a mother. I had a mom. I just wanted my story.

A few years later, I wrote her a letter saying that I came from a family of lawyers and storytellers and that I didn't believe the story she had told me. I told her I believed that she was my birth mother. That the high school picture I had of her looked so much like me—we had the same steep cheekbones, the same light eyes, the same overlapping incisor. I included a photograph of me holding Keats in the hope that my daughter's sweet little face would melt her heart. She not only had a daughter—she had a beautiful granddaughter!

I received a letter in response. Yes, she said, I was right. She was my birth mother. But, she said, it had been a closed adoption and good people had adopted me. *You have a good life,* she wrote. *Please don't contact me again*. And that was the end. No mention of Keats. No mention of loving me. Of missing me. Of wishing she could have kept me.

A couple of years later, I was talking to a friend. "That's bullshit," she said when I told her of my birth mother's dismissal. I told her the search agency had said that Beth had two sons. That meant I had two half-brothers. "Tell her you want to contact your brothers," my friend said.

"I can't do that," I said.

"Why?"

"I don't have the right." As soon as I said it, I realized I how crazy that was. "Shoot. Okay. I'll try."

I looked her up on the internet and found her work email. I wrote down the address on a scrap of paper, put it in my pocket, and took my daughter to the local Borders.

As Keats sat on the floor reading Junie B. Jones books to herself, I emailed Beth. "I understand you don't want to talk to me," I wrote on my Blackberry. "I would like to talk to your sons. Could you please give me their contact information?"

Minutes later, I got a furious email in response. "This was a closed adoption. You are invading my privacy."

"I hadn't signed anything," I wrote. "I hadn't agreed to the closed adoption. If you don't want me to contact your sons, then fine, I won't—in exchange for the true story of my birth."

A few minutes later I got an email. "I'll tell you," she said. "But then I don't want you to ever contact me again. Or my sons."

"Agreed," I wrote.

"He was someone I met at a party," she wrote. "I guess they call it date rape these days. I don't remember his name or anything about him. I decided to give life to you and you went to good parents. Please don't contact me again."

Date rape. That made so much sense to me. Maybe that was what fueled the inner fury that burned in my guts most of the time. I was born of violence. She had never wanted me.

The other possibility in the story was that she was lying because she'd had sex when she'd been drinking and, in 1964, good girls didn't do that. Date rape is so complicated. Suddenly I had to rethink sexual violence.

I was in the music section of Borders; I could look over the rows of CD's and see the children's section. I couldn't see Keats as she was sitting in between the shelves, but I could see that no one was standing there, no weird man, no body snatching woman, and so even though I couldn't see my daughter, even though I wasn't 100% sure she was okay, I stood and looked at the cover to the Cure's album with the three green palm trees and the pink pyramid, blue sky and yellow sun. I loved how it looked like someone had made the picture by cutting out pieces of construction paper. It made me feel like anything was possible. All it took was paper and scissors and you could make a world.

TRICKY

While it was true that I was sitting at the dining room table with my family, it was equally true was that in a parallel universe, the universe of my imagination, I was sitting at an entirely different table with entirely different people, eating entirely different food, so it seemed pointless to give myself one hundred percent to my life because it so easily could have not existed. This parallel universe hadn't appeared in my mind because I craved escape; it appeared because it was so logical, so possible.

Psychologists see conflict as an opposition between two simultaneous but incompatible wishes or intentions that can lead to a state of emotional tension.

Emotional tension?

You want to hear about emotional tension? Ask anyone who is adopted or has an adopted person in his family, and you will more likely than not hear stories of emotional and health issues, deviant behavior, stories about an inability to follow one chosen path or relationship. You might hear about ADD, attachment disorder, self-esteem issues, suicidal thoughts, alcoholism, drug addiction, or criminal behavior. You will hear all sorts of things that, the speaker will most likely claim, have nothing to do with adoption.

But, as an adopted person, I am skeptical about the nothing to do part. I have heard too many stories to think adoption is something that happens at birth or in childhood and then fades away into *I am part of this family* with no repercussions—no emotional issues, no health issues, no fear of future abandonment, no fear of loss.

WHAT IS INSIDE

My talent in life has been to see the jewels in others and to help them articulate their deepest dreams. It started with my mother and now I do it out of habit. I look at how people hold themselves. I look at their eyes, the way their eyes move, the clarity of gaze. I listen very closely to what people say, the words they chose, the subjects they repeat, and I ask questions. I have found that there is almost no question too personal. People want to talk; they want to be uncovered. We are born mysteries: *Who will I be? What will I do?* But generally people ask others superficial questions such as *What do you drive? How do you stay so skinny? Who cuts your hair?*

People who were adopted and who don't know their birth parents are double mysteries. There is the curiousity about the self and then there is the curiousity about the roots of the self: *Who do I look like? Do I come from bankers, doctors, robbers, whores?* Adopted people aren't much different from people who aren't adopted, they just live with more questions. They are the human experience intensified.

NOT IT

I was born in New York City in 1964 to a nineteen-year-old N.Y.U. student who gave me up for adoption and went back to school to finish her education. She told the social worker that the father was a handsome 21-year-old member of the Coast Guard but that she didn't know much else other than that he was blonde, blue-eyed, tall, and in good health. She said she had met him at a party and didn't know his name.

I don't know what's true or what happens next—I was born in December but my parents didn't get me until February. I don't know where I was those first ten weeks. I have tried to tell my story, but it was so complicated I got frozen almost as soon as I started. I went to graduate school more than twenty years ago and got an M.F.A. in fiction. When I first got there, I wrote a few pages of barely-fictionalized pages about the time my mother spent in the Peace Corps, and a day after workshop one of the older students came back with Xeroxed pages from an old *Life Magazine*. "I knew I'd heard about her," he said.

There were black and white pictures of my mom in a classroom, swinging on a rope for Peace Corps training, and an article about what had happened in Nigeria. My heart raced and I felt as if he'd brought me pages of pornography.

She'd never told me she was in *Life Magazine*. I wondered what else she hadn't told me. I wanted to call her and ask questions, but then I would have had to say that I'd written about her, and that was not an option. If I wrote about her, at some point I'd have to get to the part where I said we were not related by blood and it would have been like digging up something that was supposed to remained buried, like a body.

So I had a talent for writing, but no subject. I wanted to write about my mother and myself, but because the stories were shrouded with secrecy, I didn't have the freedom or authority to write about either.

I wrote a book-length story about a soap opera actress with an eating disorder. I called it *Gilt*. My thesis advisor said it had great dialogue but that it stayed on the surface and ignored character need.

I had called it *Gilt* as a joke to myself. I felt so guilty about everything, about the person I was, but I had no idea how to talk about something like that, and so I made guilt into gilt and wrote about a character who was a parody of a human being, a soap opera actress.

If I hadn't developed my own character, how could I develop someone else's? I was fascinated by eating disorders because of my own, but I stood at a distance from the real issues and created a character who was two dimensional because I was too afraid to really look at what it felt like to have serious issues with food. My character told jokes through her tears, skated over the surface of her days.

That description summed up my life for the next couple of decades. And then my mother died, my second marriage fell apart, I got fired for throwing a pen at a student, my daughter left for college, and I got dumped by an aging hippie. I could no longer stay on the surface because it had disappeared.

STORY

You may wonder why telling my story is so important to me. It's just story anyway, right? The great thing about being adopted, you say, is that I get to make it up. I can be whoever I want to be, and you are right. But for some reason, I am stuck. The two things I most want to do: write a book and be married are these dual mountains that I have been trying to scale my adult life only to slide right back to the ground.

I had a dream a long time ago that I was doing a reading from my recently published book and that a man was sitting in the audience and we connected glances and it was love. And, always, the way to my mother's heart was to show her a beautifully written sentence, so for a long time, I've associated writing with love. I have to do one to get the other.

How can I find love if I can't even find myself?

SHELLAC

I knew no one cleanly, wholly. My mother had the life that she lived in front of us and then the one that was in her face when she smoked her cigarettes. My good friend, in her desire to please everyone, was a chronic liar. I learned if life wasn't the way you wanted, you just said what you wanted to be true. If your mother asked if you did your homework, you said yes. If you were asked if you were angry, you said no. That fit with the life that I knew—I was a lie anyway—people called me Anne but that wasn't even my real name. I mean, it was my name, but it wasn't my only name, if I was perfectly honest about it. It wasn't the name I was given at birth.

BOO

I could have been anyone. I could have been some dark-haired heavy-set girl who hated to read and my mother would have been whispering she loved her most of all into that girl's ear. It struck me as incredibly sad that the person my mother claimed to love most in the world was interchangeable, and so I didn't trust her affection. She didn't love *me*, she loved the space I occupied. When she went to adopt a baby she hadn't asked for *me*, she had asked for a baby— anything, any color, either sex, as long as it was healthy.

I know that one could argue that this is true for any of us, no matter how we come to our parents. Our parents couldn't ask for any of us specifically. We still come out into the world as individuals, a kind of genetic crap shoot.

But children born to their parents were created while adoptees were chosen, and the problem there is that in order to be chosen we first had to be *unchosen*. The fact of the matter is that it's hard not to take being given up by your mother personally. Even if you did end up having a much better life than you would have had if she'd kept you. Even if she was twelve or had been raped or was so poor she couldn't buy herself shoes. She was still your mom, and she still chose to let you go. There must be something seriously wrong with you for your own mother to give you up because even when things get really hard most people hang on to the things they love most. Are you following this? Can you see the logic?

I'm not saying that it is a healthy or even good use of one's brain, but I am saying that if the mom I had grown up with had been the mom who had given birth to me, I'm pretty sure I wouldn't have the same glitch in my noggin that tells me I'm not valuable.

What does valuable even mean? It means worth protecting, worth keeping alive. It means that sometimes I cross the street without looking both ways because I don't care if someone hits me.

It means it's an effort to pretend I am of value, to not walk alone in a city late at night or to ask a taxi driver to slow down when it is clear he might kill me on the next turn, when my brain is telling me *you don't matter—the people who made you didn't even want you.*

Maybe you weren't even born, my beleaguered brain tells me. My story starts "The day we got you" when everyone else I know has a story that starts "The day you were born." I am a floater on this planet. Someone let go of my string a long time ago.

And why does all of this mind play matter so much to me?

Because I am 51 years old and I don't trust that anyone really loves me. I'm afraid I will never really love anyone in a way that is healthy and unconditional. I thought I loved my daughter this way, and then she left for college and it was like she disappeared. I'm afraid that my daughter will drift from me as an adult and not need me, not care if she ever sees me again. If I am really honest, I'm also afraid that I will drift from her. I'm afraid there is something so broken in me that I am capable of that. I am afraid I will never have a romantic partner whom I don't leave and who won't leave me. I'm afraid that at any minute I could turn on any of my friends and decide I don't need them anymore, and walk away. I've done it so many times. I walk away and think I am fine, and then grief sweeps in and my heart breaks and I realize, yet again, I left behind what I loved.

There is the flip side of this where I am filled with fury because I know how valuable I am. I know how ridiculous this kind of thinking and behavior is, and I am not in control. I'm a reasonable adult with a crazy child inside of her, and I want stop moving and feel at home in the world. I want to get rid of this habit of thinking of myself as someone who wasn't wanted.

TATTOO

After my mother died, I looked for the letters she had sent me over my lifetime. I could envision them: typed pages with her handwritten "love, mom" at the end, but I couldn't find any of them in my files. I just assumed they would be there. It meant something that my grammar-obsessed mother didn't capitalize the M in her name when she wrote to me. She was *mom* and I loved the casualness, the fact that she was willing to let go of a rule to show me who she was with me.

I got a pen and started writing "love" on a piece of paper, trying to get the slant and elegant sparseness of her lettering right, the L a lean loop, the o and v almost touching. I'm not sure when it started, maybe in college, but her handwriting would show up in my handwriting and there it would be, my mother's hand in my words. It's like when you look in the mirror and get a glimpse of your brother or your cousin in your own face, the shock of the realization that the river of your family runs through you.

When it looked as if my mother had written "love" all over the paper, I took the pen and wrote it on my wrist. I wanted to drag my sleeve over my hand when I went to Whole Foods for lunch, but I thought that if love was what I wanted, I should have the courage to show the world.

A week later I was in a small tattoo parlor in San Francisco getting the word bled blue into my skin. It didn't even hurt. It just lightly scabbed and then, there it was, my mother's hand on my wrist, signing off.

She would have hated the tattoo, averted her eyes. I can hear her voice now, "Oh, Anne," but I'm not listening so much anymore. It takes work, but I am pushing her voice away even as I bring her closer to my heart.

Writing is hard. Writing when you are adopted is even harder. If you think your voice is dangerous in its ability to hurt the ones you love, you learn to keep it quiet. And then the real trouble starts.

ROB

"I'm so sick of all your excuses. You are fifty years old," Rob said as he reached for the door. "You should be over the adoption thing by now."

I froze.

He was the one who was reading *Healing Childhood Wounds*. He was the one who had told me on our first date that he'd been molested, repeatedly, as a young boy, and so I had told him my feelings about being adopted, about my fears that I would never be able to grow roots of my own without habitually ripping them out. I thought it meant we were in this together, that things had happened to both of us in the past, but that with awareness and love we could overcome anything.

When he off-handedly remarked that he had a slight attachment disorder I had nodded. My therapist had once said the same thing about me. I didn't even know what it meant. I figured we were like weak Velcro, but I was always up for a good challenge. If he was going to have trouble sticking to me, I was going to work twice as hard to make myself stickable.

But now he could go fuck himself. My issues with adoption were sacred. As someone who dreamed of being a writer, they were all I had. I'd been saying for years that the one thing I knew for sure was that if I were to die that day, the one thing I would regret was that I hadn't written a book about adoption. I felt I'd been born to write about it, I just didn't know how to do it without hurting the people involved. "That's it," I said. "Get out."

"My pleasure," he said, and with that, he was gone.

I took a deep breath and put my hands on my stomach to make sure I was still there.

We were going to move in together. He'd written an email just weeks earlier: *If things go as well as they are going, which I anticipate they will, would you consider living with me? It could be your writing space. You'd have plenty of alone time. You could do massage in my office. The opportunities for us are endless.*

I had no real job to speak of, a daughter who was away at college, and one ex- and one soon to be ex-husband. I was rapidly aging, had sun spots on my face and arms, had back pain for the first time in my life, had dropped out of massage school halfway into the program, loved no one or nothing aside from my daughter with a seething passion, and had lost my mother to pancreatic cancer four years earlier. I'd also lost my birth mother to lymphoma a year prior to that, but that didn't hurt much at all.

I didn't even have a normal apartment—I was renting a room with a concrete floor in the basement of a house, a four-hundred square foot space for which I paid $1,500 a month. Thinking about all that money and the fact that I didn't even have a kitchen made me sick. My life was closing in on me because of all the choices I had made, and now even someone I had been settling for didn't think I was good enough.

Even my hair was wrong. I'd cut it short and had the fake blonde darkened when my soon to be ex-husband had his lawyer subpoena me for a deposition the week before I started massage school. I figured if he wanted to sit across the table and watch his lawyer grill me about things I had bought in the last year and pester me as to why I still didn't have a full-time job he could see my whole sleep-deprived face. I didn't want anything soft or girly on display for him, so I had my hair cut like I was two months out of the military and darkened so I looked and felt depressed.

The divorce proceedings were torturous. We'd tried to stay married, but because of our separate life experiences we were both hardwired to expect the other person to disappoint or abandon, and so we weren't able to see each other in a clear light of truth, to love unconditionally, to be in the same room together without sinking into argument, and our marriage had been more of a battle ground that anything else, and both of us were left wounded.

MOVIE PREMEIRE

To top it all off, I was in a fight with my writing partner. I'd told her I never wanted to talk to her again a month earlier, the night before our movie *Phantom Halo* premiered in San Jose. We often fought and it was always about petty things. What we didn't know how to say was, *You mean so much to me and please don't leave,* and so we pushed each other instead, again and again, testing the limits of each other's acceptance and love.

I hated that she thought she was the boss of me, but it was my own fault. We had been writing together for years, and she always had the final say. I'd let myself become subservient because I didn't believe in the power of my own voice.

BUST OUT

I'd told my friends that I was in the process of becoming a butterfly now that my second husband and I weren't together any more, that this room was my chrysalis and it was where I could safely metamorphose into my true self, but what I saw now was that really what this room was was an increasingly intense rejection of my life: a rejection of things, people, and dreams I'd collected in the last fifty years and then methodically thrown out the window one right after the other in the past year, and that the truth was that really I had created a pressing room of failure and isolation for myself, and the more I pushed people away, the more I said no to this and no to that, the smaller my space would become until I finally disappeared into the pressurized cabin of why bother.

I got a beer out of the refrigerator in the laundry room and sat down on the floor next to my bed. I wasn't a big drinker, but I was going to sit there and drink until something good happened.

I thought about how the problem was that I was adopted and hard-wired for abandonment. I knew this in my bones even if everyone around me was saying I was wrong. If I ever brought up the idea that perhaps adoption was the root cause of problems I was having—problems staying in relationships, problems with self-esteem, problems even with my digestion—people were always quick to dismiss the idea. It was like I was blaming depression on having had plastic bottles instead of glass: 1. How could I even remember and 2. That was so long ago. 3. It's not cool to play the victim. I was so sick of apologizing for my feelings and my behaviors and myself. I'd tried my whole life to be someone others would accept when, at the end, I didn't feel acceptable to myself. I couldn't do it anymore.

I went to get a second beer and sat back down, staring at the titles of the books in my bookcase: *Pilgrim at Tinker's Creek, In the Heart of the Heart of the Country, How to Not Be Yourself, Anatomy of Yoga*, and three rows of cookbooks, none of which I had touched since I had moved in. I had been surrounded by books my whole life. I may have stopped going to church when I was young, but I never stopped reading.

My phone binged with a message and I jumped, hoping it was Rob saying he'd realized his mistake and was headed back to me, but it was the chiropractor I rented a room from to do massage. "I been thinking. U need to write with Antonia. U are too talented to stop now."

I threw the phone onto my bed. On top of all of this I was supposed to think about Antonia?

The beer was working and I couldn't feel my face. I knew because I lightly slapped it. It was so satisfying not to feel I slapped it a number of times.

My life without Antonia was not as good as it was with her. I didn't have the hope that every day she might text me that someone wonderful was reading a script of ours, that our ship had come in, that the movie we'd co-written and she had directed was on some best seller list and that someone at Sony or Universal wanted to hire us to clean up someone else's script. Mostly I didn't have someone I called my best friend, my sister, someone with whom I talked about my life, and who seemed always to be in the exact same place in her life's voyage that I was. We'd lost our mothers within a year of each other, and that, if nothing else, had made us close.

I was lucky she stuck with me. Half the time I couldn't even remember the story line when we were writing because I felt like I was treading water, unable to get into the truth of what I really wanted to say.

I rolled over on the floor and pulled my phone off the bed. "I miss you," I texted to Antonia. "Dr. Mark says that we need to be writing together."

I pressed send and looked heavenward, fake praying. I had told Antonia I didn't want to ever talk to her again when she had told me I shouldn't have said something in an interview. I had told her to fuck off.

My phone dinged almost immediately. "Yay!" she had written.

It dinged again. "I'm in Poland meeting with a director here. I'll be back Monday. Let's start writing again then."

I couldn't believe it. The partnership wasn't dead. It had survived yet another major battle and now we were going to get back together and have another chance to make a movie.

I texted my usual "xxx" and lay back down. It felt good to have the floor behind me. I wished the ceiling would lower and offer the same kind of solid support, so I could be the protected filling of a room Oreo cookie. As is was, my front side felt exposed, like a clam belly without its top shell.

Being single was so lonely. I felt exposed, vulnerable to disaster. Who would take me to the hospital if my gallbladder burst?

Who would be there to sit next to me at the movies? Who would be there at Christmas?

I wished Rob would come back to my door. I wished he would knock on the glass lightly, hoping I would let him in. If he did, I would embrace him and whisper in his ear that I loved him and never let him go. I had been hasty in judging him. It wasn't right to think I was better than he was. I was in danger of spending the rest of my life alone if I didn't learn to be more flexible and understanding.

Even more, because he probably wouldn't talk as incessantly as Rob did, I wished Jesus could come down from the heavens above and fill my body with light and goodness, but when I closed my eyes and waited for enlightenment, nothing happened.

MY HERO

A few years earlier my half-brother, whom I had never met, got in his car and drove down from his temporary work site in San Francisco to come meet me. He may as well have come cantering up on a white horse. Having someone claim you is the bomb.

MOVIES ARE BETTER

Ready to grovel, I drove up Rob's driveway, and he was still sitting outside in his chair in his teaching clothes—his khaki pants and his striped shirt. He looked up from his phone and there was no expression on his face. I wished he would smile.

I got out of my car and walked over to him.

"Hello," he said.

"I couldn't let it end like that," I said. "It didn't feel right."

I sat at the plastic picnic table and faced him.

I took a deep breath and felt like I was loading a gun of my will. "I'm convinced I can love you the way you need to be loved. I can love you like no one else has. Not your mom, your dad, your previous wives. I see you. I know you need someone to stand by you, to be faithful, to adore you. I can do that, but I'm going to make mistakes. You have to bear with me, talk it through."

Rob's face didn't change at all, but I saw a tear catch on the edge of his glasses. "I want that," he said.

What I learned when I went deep sea fishing is that when you have a fish on the line you don't reel it in as fast as you can. You have to focus on slowly drawing in the line so as not to rip the hook out of its mouth.

I took a deep breath, smiled.

"I love you," I said.

"You need to be grateful for your adoption," Rob said. "You are lucky you got the parents you did. Your adoptive parents are good to you."

His arms were thinner than mine and his pants were stained.

I stood up, walked to my car, and drove away.

DADDY

When you are a woman who is adopted and who doesn't know all the facts of her origin, you can look at the man you are dating and wonder if he is either your brother or father. It lends for a strange intimacy and distance at the same time.

I remember as a kid realizing that, technically, I could marry my brothers, my cousins, my uncles, my father (!) since we weren't related by blood. It made the world ridiculous, that fundamental laws the rest of the world had to follow didn't exactly apply to me. I looked normal, but I was a maelstrom in the making. All I had to do was to step into what was possible, and the normal world would crumble.

DONER

Not atypically, I only became curious about who my birth father was when I had a baby of my own. He hadn't even registered in my consciousness. I had a father. Why this same logic didn't work for my mother, I'm not sure. Maybe it has to do with the immediacy of flesh. The birth mother is the doorway to life. The father is more like the postman.

GET ME OUT OF HERE

One time, one terrible time, we went to a family counselor when I was a teenager. After a while, near the end of the session the balding, sweating therapist said, "Well, we've covered the problems the two boys are having, what about Anne?" and I froze, afraid to hear my parents' litany of complaints. My father choked up and said, "When Anne walks in the room, everyone relaxes." I felt proud and awful at the same time. I was still the good kid, but the only problem was that I hated everyone in the room. They were my family, but they were the *wrong* family and there was nothing I could do about that. I was completely powerless.

My father said he wished that he and I spent more time together. I was horrified because my father looked so sad and spending time with him was not an option—I could barely look at him while he sat there. Our family dynamics were that my mother told me how my father failed her and it was my job to express anger at him because she couldn't.

My father was a good guy: honest, smart, kind, and he had no trouble talking to me about adoption, which was good. I didn't have to worry about hurting his feelings. But I was my mother's child first and foremost, and if he wasn't making her happy, if he wasn't earning enough money; if he was sitting around while she cleaned, he was going to have to answer to me.

THE WIND IT WILL BLOW

Many people I've talked to think being adopted might be a

wonderful out. They dream of being told they are adopted, of being told that truly they aren't like their crazy parents, their annoying siblings. It would be like a get out of jail free card for them. They wouldn't feel bound by the genetics they feel imprisoned by. They would be free.

I get it. A tree planted by the highway might dream of being a tree by the beach, but it is hindered by roots. Tear out the roots and set it by the beach and then it is a post.

Free, but unsteady.

SNORT

There's a popular children's book from 1960 called *Are You My Mother?* It's the one where the mother bird flies off to get food before the baby bird hatches. The baby says "Where is my mother?" and hops out of the nest in search of her. He asks a kitten, a hen, a dog, a cow and finally a steam shovel it calls Snort if they are his mother. The steam shovel lifts the baby bird back to his nest as the mother bird arrives with a worm. "I know who you are," the baby bird says. "You are not a kitten or a hen or a dog. You are not a cow or a

Snort. You are a bird, and you are my mother!"

And that's it. A baby bird goes in search of his lost mother and finds her. This simple story written in the 1960's has sold over ten million copies. It was voted one of the top 100 picture books of all time by the School Library Journal.

This book has remained popular for all these years for a reason: people empathize with the baby bird. Of course it wants to find its mother. We want to know our origins. And, more simply: we want to find our mothers.

BEGINNINGS

Why do people rush to get to movies on time? What's the big deal about starting fifteen minutes into the show? Because no one wants to miss the beginning. In order to understand the ending, you generally need to see the beginning. In order to understand yourself, if you are a baby bird, you need to see that you came from a mama bird, not a steam shovel.

And this is true, I believe, for most children who are adopted.

And why I am making such a big deal of all this? All my life,

I have had the feeling that something was wrong, but I couldn't figure out what it was. In my teens I finally decided it was me. I went to therapists and doctors in search of ways to feel better. I suffered from depression, eating disorders, an inability to stick with jobs, schools, people.

We rarely talked about adoption. It would come up, and the standard response was "How old were you?" I would say, "Ten weeks," and we would both shrug like, oh, it's just a paper cut. The next question that wasn't really a question was almost always, "But good people adopted you, right?" and I would nod.

I could no more say anything negative about whom I had been given as parents than I could curse God. I could do it, but the risk was unfathomable. It didn't even matter whether I was a believer: there was still the chance that the skies would open and the wrath of the universe would descend upon me and I would disappear. Or that I would just make my parents really, really sad if they ever found out I had said negative things about them.

So, "Yes," I would say. "Good people adopted me," and then we would move on and talk about everything else that was happening in my life that might be the cause of my troubles.

But, for a minute, follow me:

A man and a woman come together and a sperm worms its way into an egg, and that is the start of you. You split and split and a heart forms and a brain stem and then your fingers are moving and you touch the walls of your home. You grab hold of the cord that connects you to your home. You lick the walls. You smell the warm fluid that is your home. You listen to the beat of home, to the sounds that come from above, voice and heartbeat and, perhaps, song. There is no separation between you and the walls around you. You are all one growing thing. And then the squeezing starts and space turns into no space.

The light is shocking. Everything you knew has disappeared and softness has turned to edges and things that hurt. You cry. There is something you need, your body moves towards it like a plant to the sun, but it's not there. The yearning pulls you to home, but you are carried away. Everything is not it, not it, not it, and then you forget, you almost all the way forget, but a part of you is always searching.

BEGINNINGS KEEP HAPPENING

The baby is adaptable, and it eats and sleeps and smiles and laughs and cries like a normal baby, but maybe there is an uneasy hole of longing in its gut, so maybe it eats a little more than other babies, drinks from its bottle more rapidly. Maybe it falls in love with anyone who comes into its vision because, when you are drowning, you will hold onto anything. It looks like a normal baby—it's got all its parts, and when the court gives it to a new set of parents, it becomes a new baby. It gets a new name, a new birth certificate. It has a new story of origin, and this story begins, *The day we got you.*

Just for the heck of it, let's play pretend:

Go under water and come back to the surface in ten weeks. Go to China and come back in ten weeks. Go to outer space in a rocket and come back in ten weeks. Go to your own backyard and climb up a tree and come back down in ten weeks. No big deal, right? It'd be like nothing ever happened.

Don't be ridiculous you tell me. I'm an adult, of course those things will be monumental, you say, but it's different when you are newly born. You don't remember.

Okay, then. Go to the hospital and have a baby and kiss her on the wet head and say, *See you in ten weeks*, and then go home. Pick her up after the time has passed and bring her back and tell me you think she would be exactly the same child if you had held on to her. Have a baby and see for yourself if it's no big deal. It could be a real bonus for you to not after deal with those first weeks of sleepless nights, constant feedings.

When I was pregnant, I thought there was a fish in me. How could someone who had no story of her birth could give birth herself? The only name I had to suggest was Hammerhead Shark; luckily my husband came up with something better.

Right after my daughter was born, there was concern because she was yellowish, and the doctor lay her on a bed next to my bed for further examination, and my daughter was naked and crying. I reached over to touch her, and as soon as my fingertip grazed her arm, she quieted. To me, that was the first moment of mothering, and it was powerful. I was there to make her feel safe, and she felt it, and the bond between us was strong.

I think about how her dad and I took turns holding her those first days, weeks, months. How she would fall asleep on one of us as we lay on the couch, trying for a few z's ourselves. How we would repeatedly stand at the edge of her bassinette, checking that her chest was actually rising and falling, checking that was she truly sleeping and not dead. I think about how we would talk to her, sing to her, play with her rubbery arms and legs.

And so when people say, "Oh, you were a baby," when I say I was adopted at ten weeks, I find it hard to believe that really—even though I have no memories of that time, not even shadow memories—those first ten weeks didn't count.

MOTHER ON FIRE

When I was eighteen and a freshman at Kenyon College, my English teacher had us write an essay in response to reading Virginia Woolf's *A Room of One's Own*. I wrote about my mother's attempt to create a space of her own in our house where she could work, the coat closet she had converted into an office.

I wrote about how it was my job to try to keep my brothers from knocking on the door and disturbing her. I wrote about how frustrated she would get because my brothers were unrelenting. She worked as a stringer for the local paper when I was in junior high. She would type and smoke cigarettes during the afternoons, and I wrote about how the smoke would leak out from under the door until it looked as if my mother was on fire. There was never enough time, never enough money, never enough privacy for her, and I had the constant sense that I was letting her down.

I wrote in the essay how it wasn't enough for a woman to have a room of her own. I wrote about the importance of having the time to be in that room and the importance of having a lock on the door. I wrote about how, as a family, we were letting my mother down and how, really, she was letting herself down by putting a higher priority on cooking mediocre dinners for us before writing the book she said she wanted to write, a biography of Louisa Adams, whose portrait my mother had fallen in love with during a visit to the Quincy Family Museum in the 1970's.

My teacher gave me an A, photocopied the essay, and handed it out to the class. I was proud, but I was drawing aside the curtain on my mother's life, and I so most of all I was ashamed I had talked about what was supposed to stay unexamined: the fact that my mother, who liked to present herself as happy and unstoppable, was failing to live the life of her dreams.

I SEE YOU

No one knew my mother like I did. No one studied her like I did. I knew my mother's potential. I knew what she was supposed to be: a famous writer who was in *The New Yorker*, not a distracted housewife and part time stringer for the local paper who read *Talk of the Town* on the toilet.

I kept telling her she needed to find time to write her book. I told her my father should chip in and cook meals even though he moved about the kitchen like everything was sharp. I became the house shrew, scolding my father and brothers, trying to herd them into obedience. I felt like I was in the driver's seat in her life, but the steering wheel didn't work. I saw exactly where the car was supposed to go, but I couldn't get it to change direction.

I'd put the Beatles album on while we cleaned the house on Saturdays and play *Paperback Writer* repeatedly until my mother told me enough was enough. She was too busy to write a book. She needed to get the house cleaned and dinner made so she could have time to work in her garden, and if I really wanted to be a help I could go to the basement and get the vacuum.

WHAT IS IT?

I'd never had a problem making friends until I left home and went to Kenyon, and it soon became clear that the skills I'd had to make my close friends at home didn't work in Gambier, Ohio. I felt like a piece of tape that had lost its stick. I still looked like tape, still felt like tape—I just couldn't figure out where the stick had gone or why. What was wrong with me? Why didn't I have the same kind of friends that I had had back home?

I'd grown up feeling mildly like an outsider, but I'd always managed to be surrounded by friends. I knew there was something slightly off about me, and I suspected that either I wasn't quite pretty enough or smart enough or that somehow because I was part of a family that looked dysfunctional compared to other families around that this put me in a special group of people, those who didn't quite work right in the world.

At Kenyon I was no one's best friend, and although there was a pack of us who ate every night at the dining hall and went to parties together, I wasn't essential in anyone's life there and by the end of freshman year, people were arranging their next year's roommates, and no one asked me. I decided the problem was that I was too far from my family, too far from what was familiar, so I decided to leave. The best course of action seemed to be to give up trying to carve out my own path and to follow my mother's.

I transferred to Smith, her alma mater. When I was getting ready to go, my grandmother went into her attic and pulled out the thigh-length raccoon coat my mother had worn when she was a freshman, and I wore it with great pride. Like my mother, like Sylvia Plath, I would be a "Smithie" with the whole world in front of me. According to my mother I would become a powerful woman with unlimited potential. I went to Boston and spent a big chunk of my waitressing money on a haircut so I could fit in the with other girls I'd seen at my visit to Smith with their edgy haircuts, sticky with pomade.

I lasted ten days before I got on my bike looking for the Mass Pike, looking for home. I'd found out that it wasn't Kenyon or Ohio that was the problem: it was me. I still didn't fit in. I still wasn't attracting friends who weren't somehow on the fringe.

I had no idea who I was. I had grown up thinking I was a

fairly normal girl who did pretty well in life, but suddenly I was flailing, and I didn't know why. I was some girl who went to get ice cream twice a day because she was so empty.

I got lost on my search for the Mass Pike and called my parents from a liquor store payphone on a country road. "Don't sign anything," my mother said as I sobbed my plight to them, but it was too late. I'd met with the dean and signed my withdrawal papers. I'd gone to the bookstore and had the cash for the returned books in my pocket. My father came to Smith that night and brought me back home, but my mother wasn't there to greet me. She didn't come out of her room for three days. She'd been thrilled that her daughter was following in her footsteps, and now the bubble was burst and she couldn't bear to look at me.

I went into a quiet tailspin. I got a job as a waitress in Faneuil Hall and got fired after an hour for not knowing what went into a Bloody Mary. My mother had expected me to fail if I wasn't in college, and I was failing. I felt like Sisyphus, carrying someone else's dreams on my back until they got too heavy and I rolled back down to the bottom of the mountain. I was trying to be myself and the person my mother wanted at the same time and it just wasn't working.

It was like I was in a boxing ring, trying to knock myself out.

I ended up getting a 9-5 job doing data entry. Brokers would call and read CUSIP numbers for stocks and bonds, and I would type in the numbers and say if they were clear or not. If I remember correctly, they were always clear. I worked as a bar back three nights a week at a local restaurant. I spent whatever money I made as fast as I made it.

IT TOOK YOU LONG ENOUGH

When I was a child, we had wonderful family vacations with friends at their Martha's Vineyard house. There was a converted chicken coop across the dirt road, and I would occasionally get up early and stand on the wooden fence and watch the hippies come out of the tiny house and stretch themselves to a good morning. It was the early seventies, and these hippies were the real deal: skinny and wild. I wanted to be as fearlessly my own person as they were.

Thirty years later I wrote a screenplay based on my running away from Smith, only I had the main character end up on Martha's Vineyard where she got a job selling fish and lived in a converted chicken coop. The problem with the screenplay was that it didn't have a real plot because I didn't write much about the conflict the young woman (me) had with her mother.

It was another five years after that I ending up going to Martha's Vineyard as part of Write or Die: I had run away from my life again, only this time I did it right: I wrote the story and looked my relationship with my mother in the face. I went wild hippie on myself.

MOMS ARE CONFUSING

I was shocked and heartbroken when she refused to come out of her room to see me after I left Smith, but I pretended I was okay and focused on getting a job at a bar in Faneuil Hall, a job that had seemed romantic and exciting to me when I'd been back at Smith, dreaming about a life that was mine, not a copy of my mother's.

I bounced back and forth from thinking I was a carbon copy of my mother: smart, bookish, slightly socially awkward, and shy, to thinking that I was the opposite: a raucous girl with a loud laugh who ran with the boy she liked in the middle of the night and who was always the first to dive into the pool fully dressed at a party. Both personalities made me feel uncomfortable and misunderstood—the first made me feel safe but small and the second made me feel ashamed, too big and out of control for my parents to handle.

My mother wore Lee jeans with sweaters and turtlenecks. She didn't have pierced ears. She never dyed her hair or put any real effort into making the most of her femininity. She would polish her nails but then quickly chip the paint gardening without gloves. She smoked, and her teeth were yellowed and her lips were almost always chapped. She had perfect eyebrows, a patrician profile, and in photographs from the 1960's, she reminded me of Sylvia Plath or Jackie Onassis, leanly elegant women with smiling mouths and eyes that were focused inwardly, listening to their own thoughts while pretending to attend to the outside world.

There was a sadness in my mother, something unreachable, and she was like a magnet to me. The problem was that when she touched me, it usually hurt. Her fingers were long and thin and it seemed like she didn't have full awareness of where they were. She would poke me, scratch me with her ragged nails, mistakenly touch my breast instead of my shoulder. I'd feel invaded and angry at her, but also at myself for being so impatient. I'd retreat to my room and hope that next time might be better.

She confided her unhappiness to me, her belief that my father had failed as a provider, her fears about my brothers and the trouble they fell into, her fear that we didn't have enough money to buy the things we needed as family: groceries, clothes, vet care for our cats and dog, a roof that wasn't threatening collapse.

DROP OUT

In my early twenties, I dropped out of college for the third time and decided to make a living waiting tables. The visiting writer at Occidental had pushed a two-page story I'd written for class back at me during our one-on-one meeting. "You're a writer," he'd said through his busted up teeth. "You don't need me." I figured I could write a book during my off hours and make all my dreams come true, mostly that I'd be famous and have nice clothes and clever friends and be thin and finally have a real boyfriend.

I took my teacher literally and dropped out of school the next day. When I finally worked up the courage to tell my mother what I had done, she wept over the phone. "What will I tell my friends?" she said.

"You can tell them I'm waiting tables in L.A. and writing."

My mother made a choking noise. "I have to go," she said. "This is too hard for me to talk about right now."

I felt desperate enough to lift the robes on my ambition. "I think I'm supposed to write a book, Mom. My teacher told me I'm a good writer. I don't need school for that."

"What will you even write about?"

I covered my eyes so I didn't have to watch myself have this conversation. "My life, I guess."

"You mean autobiography?"

"Well, yeah. It's what I know." I had taken an autobiography class at Occidental. We read Bell Hooks, Jean Genet, Alice Walker, Ben Franklin. Proust. Everyone had his story, and it didn't have to be big, it just had to be specific and interesting and beautifully written. Genet wrote about the worm of Vaseline emerging as he squeezed the tube before having sex with another man. Proust wrote about madeleines and memories. Cookies. The guy had written about cookies and was famous all over the world. Why couldn't I do something similar?

Each of these authors had a reason for writing autobiography, a specific point of view that ideally helped open a new window of insight for the reader. But none of these writers were adopted as far as I knew. I had my own story—I had a *subject*, if only I could find a way to tell it.

None of these writers, I imagined, felt compelled to get their mother's permission before they spilled themselves on the page. Joseph Campbell never talked about the compulsion of getting your mother's permission to go out into the world and be yourself. I was going to have to hack out that path on my own.

I was also going to have to ask her to help me pay the rent for the first few months before I got enough hours at the restaurant to make ends meet, so I had to make her believe in my plan.

My path was clear to me—like my mother, it was my destiny to be writer, but unlike her I was going to do something about it. I just needed her support.

"But your experiences don't necessarily add up to a book."

"Isn't that defeatist?" I didn't normally challenge her like this, but I was tired of her pushing me down while claiming to offer support. There was so much my mother didn't know. She thought I was a good girl. She thought I was like her, and that, like her, I would edit whatever stories I did have until there was little left to tell.

She paused and for a moment I had the strange feeling that she had silently hung up the phone and that I had finally done it, finally crossed the line I'd been looking for my whole life. The line between I am your mother and that's it, I'm done with this charade.

When she spoke I felt both great relief and disappointment. "It's realistic. A college degree is the foundation for everything," she said. "You can write a book when you graduate."

"But you didn't."

"That's not fair. I did other things."

"A person can die from doing what she's supposed to."

"This is too much for me, Honey. I have a lot to do and this is very draining."

I was obsessed with the book *The Hero with a Thousand Faces* after finding it in a library cubicle, and it was my belief that for me to be the hero of my life, I had to break away from the narrative my parents had provided for me and find my own path. I just needed my mother to believe in me so she would help finance it.

"Mom?"

"Yes."

"I think I have to do this. It doesn't even feel like a choice."

"I understand you feel this way, but it is a choice. I have to argue that what you need to do is to make a commitment and stick with it."

My mother was supportive until she was tired or angry, and then her real thoughts would leak out. I had learned to watch for the actions behind the actions because I saw that she was a paper doll standing in front of a bruise of disappointment and anger. I would watch her smoke her cigarettes, and I would see the truth of her feelings in the burn of paper and tobacco. She would exhale and I would know that she was there, somewhere, in the disappearing grey smoke. As a child, I felt so lonely watching my mother smoke. She was a million miles away.

I pushed my fingers into my closed eyes. I'd worked at Friendly's all summer and had bought a car and driven to L.A. on my own. My parents had told me to call them when I got to Occidental, and I had done it. I'd left home and driven over three thousand miles by myself. I was low maintenance. None of my friends' parents would have said "Call me when you get there." Wasn't my ability to take care of myself a big deal? Wasn't that its own kind of commitment? Just because I wasn't committed to what they wanted for me didn't mean I was a failure, but sitting there on the phone with my mother I felt like one as I saw that, really, I had no path, that the brief charade of me being a writer was over.

My mother and I said goodbye without resolving anything. I was going to have to call back soon and ask for financial support. I dreaded that call.

TRIP AND FALL

I knew I was in trouble when I dropped out of college for the second time, but I had no idea how to fix what was wrong, since what was wrong was clearly me, and that wasn't something I could escape. I'd moved all the way across the country to escape myself, but all I'd done is gotten skinnier and more physically distanced from my friends and family back home.

I started spending a lot of time in the Occidental library after I dropped out, more time than I'd ever spent there when I was enrolled as a student. I tried to write, but I had nothing pressing to say besides

"I wish I were thinner," and so I got a stack of books and a notebook and decided to be an autodidact on how best to live.

Reading at a desk in the stacks made me feel like there was still hope for me, and I obsessively read about Joseph Campbell and his idea of the hero's journey. I felt I was some kind of hero in the making—I was the only one of my childhood friends or family members who had gone off the beaten path of high school to college, and I felt there had to be a reason why my life was turning out to be so different from theirs—but the problem was I had no idea what the point of my journey was or what the boon was that I would one day be bringing home with me. I was like the Easter Bunny with no basket or an arrow with no target.

It's scary to be twenty-one and to feel like a loser. One way to feel in control is to have an eating disorder, so I did that, and that took a lot of energy, living hungry, but being skinny only takes you so far, even in Los Angeles. I still didn't have a boyfriend or things aside from my low weight to feel good about. I could no longer say I was a college student, and I couldn't say I was a writer because I didn't actually write.

I felt like Ben in *The Graduate* in those scenes when he was drifting in his parents' pool. I'd gone from being a good kid to being a drifter and I couldn't seem to find my way back.

HERE I AM

When I was in graduate school I wrote a short story called *Keys*. It was about how many people's houses I had lived in other than my own, how I felt more comfortable in the home of my best friend or at my grandparents' or at a co-worker's apartment than at my own place. It was a phenomenon I couldn't explain, but it's clear to me now it is somehow linked to the trauma of adoption.

As an adopted person I am a silver ball that just happened to land on Red 9, on *Anne Heffron*. I could so easily could have landed on Black 4, *Jessica Silverstein*, say, or *Heidi Stork*. And so maybe I just keep reliving the crap shoot of my life. *Oh, here is home. Oh, here is home. And here, I am home here now.* There is a wild familiar feeling of anything is possible when I can jump from my life into someone else's. I got married twice and so twice I had a new last name.

The tricky part comes in the subconscious need to feel in control. One way to pretend that you have power in your life is to take on an identity, a place of residence, a friend, a boyfriend, a job, a school, and then to say, *This is not who I am*, and to walk away, feeling, temporarily, liberated and strong in your sense of self, which, unfortunately, is more about who you aren't than who you are and is therefore only a temporary strength. It's like this fantasy of going back in time and rejecting the birth mother before she can reject you. It's a way of reliving the past and, for a brief period of time, being the superhero of rejection instead of the object.

All my adult life I have only been able to keep up the act of being myself for so long and then I have to leave. It's like I'm a pressure cooker and at some point I think I will explode if I don't escape. This means that almost everything is temporary. I have lost count of how many jobs I have had, how many places I have lived, how many men I thought I loved. I went to five colleges. I buy things and then give them away, so I have long ago lost track of what stuff I own.

This kind of willful abandon may sound fine, a life of a gypsy, wild, untamed, untethered by expectations, but if you saw the movie

Gravity with Sandra Bullock, you'll remember the scene when she was floating in space alone, unattached to the space ship: both the audience and Sandra Bullock's character were terrified.

I wanted two things more than anything: to be alone and to not be alone. This means I have spent my life gathering people to me and then systematically shutting them out. The danger of having someone close to me, someone close enough to see me when I was too tired to do the song and dance of Anne, was that he or she would see who I really was—someone so worthless even her mother gave her away.

MUG SHOT

From what I have written so far, you might think that I am a sad sack who sighs her way through life, but the fact is that most people think I am carefree and happy. More than just about anything I like to laugh, and it's the kind of laugh makes people stop and look. It's loud. It's the laugh of a joyful person. I think that's who I am. That's the me before my brain kicks in and says I'm no good.

OM

I took a yoga workshop with Erich Schiffman once, and he talked about the idea that we think we are individual waves in the ocean, when really we are all just ocean. I loved that my sense of being separate from others was a misunderstanding, and that I was just a speck in a roiling mass of humanity, but I couldn't feel it. Even in the classroom I had put myself in the very back row so that I could feel part of the group but separate.

I don't know how to say this and not sound childlike, but I think that if I hadn't been adopted, I might have acted differently. People hate when I talk like this because I sound like I am complaining and because I am talking about something they can't fix, and so I learned early on to keep quiet about it, even to myself, but there has been a little voice in my head ever since I can remember telling me that I am different. Other people can just say who they are and know where they came from, but I had an asterisk by my name, and it told me that I wasn't like everyone else, that everyone else had come from their visible life. Do I think about this all the time? I don't think there is any one thing I think of all the time, but I do know that the fact that I am adopted comes into my mind every single day in one way or another, and that is the thing that separates me from everyone else—not the thinking—but the fact that I can't talk about the thinking because it either makes people uncomfortable, annoyed, or bored.

What if there was a special section in the yoga class for adopted people? What if they were in a little group off to the side, practicing yoga, looking at each other surreptitiously for any oddities, for any similarities: *Are we related? Are you my sister? My brother? My cousin? My dad?* I think at first I would resent being cordoned off and sent to be with the special kids, but I imagine sometime in the class I would finally catch eyes with another adopted person, and we would see each other, and we would start to laugh and we would just keep laughing because it was all so funny, our mothers couldn't keep us so we got a different mother, a new family, a new life, and look, now here we are practicing yoga and *I see you I see you I see you.* It would be such a relief. I wouldn't have to carry the adoption secret around any more like a stone in my gut. It was out there in the open, and I could laugh and cry and everyone would understand.

THE TRUTH BENDS

My mother was a writer and my father was a lawyer, and so in our house words mattered. I learned to play with language and the presentation of reality by listening to my parents talk. I learned to state the facts, but to leave out what didn't fit, to stick to the Fifth Amendment and only say what was necessary, somewhat like saying "This is my daughter." What is implied in this statement is that you gave birth to or sired that offspring. You can let the world think what it will. You didn't lie.

This made the world a watery place for me: facts were mercury—nothing was concrete. Almost anything could be true. I just had to word it correctly.

LISTEN

I taught writing for almost twenty years at the college level before I got fired for throwing a pen at a student, repeatedly saying *fuck*, and crying.

I believed in the transformative powers of writing and encouraged people to develop their voices and to tell their stories.

Sometimes I felt like a preacher in front of the class. I could see the gifts these kids carried within, and I was intent on getting them to see that, despite all the red marks and low grades they'd gotten for years in school, they could write. Anyone could write. They had to believe that what they were saying was important.

I had a football player who was set on failing my class because he'd always failed his English classes. His essays were terrible. He, like so many others, couldn't get a sentence on paper without first thinking about what he was supposed to say. That thought process killed his voice because he never even heard it, the other voices: his teachers, his parents, god knows who else, jumped all over the thought and hammered the life out of it before it had a chance to get on the page. The poor kid suffered through every essay, and then he wrote about In and Out Burger, and everything changed. "Sometimes you just got to have a juicy Double Double" he wrote, and I flipped out.

"That's your voice!" I said, pretty much jumping up and down.

He shook his head. "That's how I talk," he said. "I need to sound different when I write."

70

I stepped back and looked at him. "I am going to find all your old teachers and yell at them."

"Let me get you their addresses," he said, and we went back to work.

PERFECT STORM

How did I go from helping students to assault and battery? First of all, I have been throwing pens in class for years. I don't do it to hurt: I do it to wake up a student who is confusing me with a TV. I usually miss, and I missed the day I got fired, but this was the first time my conduct was reported. I never knew it was assault and battery. It wasn't even a pen, to be honest, it was a dry erase, but I suppose it's semantics at this point.

The student was sitting in the corner of the back of the room, where he always sat. I had let him add the class two weeks late, and he was a chatty kid, borderline rude in his cooler than you slide into the classroom every day, but I was only teaching one class and I was determined to do the best teaching job I'd ever done. The only problem was that I was going through a divorce and still grieving the death of my mother and so my brain wasn't working the way it normally did. I made my way through my days pretending drowning was really a walk in the park. I felt disoriented much of the time. I got lost easily and had a hard time looking at the clock in the classroom and knowing what it said. Basic things didn't make sense any more.

The day I got fired I had left the house with my daughter still in bed, head and body under the covers. I kissed the lump that was her and told her I would be back in a few hours. She should have been in school, but the day before she'd been rejected by the college we'd been all but assured she would attend as a student athlete, and she was heartbroken. She'd taken two of her friends that year to the hospital because of suicide scares, and I was terrified she might be next. The world seemed crazy enough those days. Anything was possible, even my stable, collected daughter could decide that life was not worth it.

In the classroom, I was teaching about writing conclusions, and this one student would not stop talking to the student next to him, even after I had asked him a number of times to be quiet or to teach the material instead of me so I could sit back there and relax. I watched him talk, and I thought about how the conclusion is such a critical part of the essay but that most everyone in the room thought the conclusion was supposed to simply repeat the introduction, and how for the rest of his life this kid was probably going to write boring conclusions because he wanted to act like a jerk in class and talk to his neighbor. I thought about how my mother was dead and how my second husband had called me names because that's what his father had done to his mother and I thought about the fact that I was standing in front of this class when I should have been back home with my daughter, snuggled up behind her, breathing into her hair until she was strong enough to get out of bed again.

When I threw the pen, I wanted to get the kid to stop talking. I wanted him to pay attention so that I could teach the lesson and then hurry home. I threw it, burst into tears, and said, "Fuck." I said "fuck" a bunch of times because throwing the pen had done nothing. The kid was still talking. But now everyone else was staring at me with concern. I felt like a tornado.

I tried to gain control, but I could not stop crying and saying fuck. Finally I got hold of myself and finished teaching. At the end of class, several students gathered around me to give me a hug. The next day I was out of a job.

BAG OF GUNS

When we first got my brother Sam, he was a little more than two years old and didn't talk. At the time, my parents attributed his silence to the double ear infection he turned out to have, but in retrospect, it makes a lot of sense to me that my brother was in shock. However, this wasn't talked about, wasn't even considered: the trauma of losing a mother and being in foster care and then getting a new mother. The focus was on what my parents could give Sam: a new bed, new toys, new clothes, new aunts, new uncles, new friends, and a white brother and sister. Change, even when it is good, is still a shock to the system. Why didn't Sam come with a manual? Why did he only arrive with the bag of toy guns he'd had in his previous life? And while we're at it, why did they give a kid of mixed race to a white family in an all-white town?

OW

It is very hard for me to write about this. My life would be easier and I would feel like a better person if I believed the story I was

74

fed as a child, as an adolescent, as an adult, that adoption is a beautiful, easy thing because, truly, in so many ways it is: one set of parents can't properly care for a child and so they find a set of parents that can. So simple. I hate being the voice of complaint, the kid waving her hand in the back of the class to say that, in fact, the desks are super uncomfortable and the angle of the seat is sure to do damage to my spine years down the road. I could go to Camp Suck It Up and make no waves, and I did, I tried to, but I can't any more. I have worked myself into a corner where I have no job, no house, no life partner, and so I have to look at what is difficult, at what I could change. I want to write the book that, if I had read it at seventeen, I wouldn't have felt so badly about myself, so wrong, so destined for a shaky future.

YOUR NAME CHANGES

We talked about his curly hair, his bag of guns, but there was no mention of where he had been, who he might have loved before he came to our house as a two year old. He had a mom now. He had a dad. He had a brother and a sister. We thought that was what mattered. My parents took us to McDonald's to celebrate Sam's arrival.

His name then was Terrence, and we called him Terry, but my parents wanted a name they felt was more befitting of a man in high position, a judge, for example, and so on his birth certificate they changed his name to Samuel Terry Heffron. During his first grade teacher conference, his teacher referred to him as Sam, and my parents told her that they were still calling him Terry. "He told me his name is Sam," the teacher said, and so that's when the name change officially happened.

I have a friend I have known since I was ten months old, and sometimes she slips and calls him Terry, but she's the only one. He's Sam now.

When I found some of his birth family online, the brother of Sam's birth father and his wife and child, they called immediately. We started excitedly exchanging information, and I told them Terry's name was Sam now and that Sam had said I could search for his family as he was ambivalent. There was silence on the other end of the line. "What was wrong with Terrence?" the woman finally asked. We were trying to like each other and I could tell she didn't want to insult me, but that she was handling the surprise the best she could. "Nothing," I told her.

"It was his father's brother's name," she said. "I mean his birth father."

"It's a great name," I told her. "I guess my parents just wanted to make him more their own."

"Sam," she said, as if trying out a new flavor of popsicle. "Okay. Sam."

BOOKS

I came with a set of books when my parents adopted me, hardbound, in a grey binder. One was for children and the other was for adults, but, with their grey covers and stiff bindings, they both seemed serious. As a child, I loved that I had arrived with books explaining my story. My friends had their parents to tell them the stories of their birth, but I had books illustrating the fact, rather than being born, I'd been chosen.

The books are gone now and I don't remember what they said, but I do remember that the illustrations were serious, elegant. This was a New York adoption agency, and the books were probably published in the 1950's or early 60's. They weren't *fun* books. They were respectful.

I went from the simple children's book of you are adopted and these are your new parents to the adult's book hoping for more, for secrets, but was faced instead with tightly packed text that was not entertaining to read and made no sense to me—like an eight year old trying to read *The Wall Street Journal*—because all I remember feeling was *this is not for me* and being disappointed. Even then, I suspected there was more to the story.

I had other paperwork that came with me with I was adopted, letters from my parents' lawyer, paperwork from the adoption agency. Some of the copied pages were on onion skin paper and I liked the fragile feel of my history. There were papers that outlined the payments my parents had made for the adoption. There was even a paper where, mistakenly, my birth name was left unaltered that I would later be able to use to locate my birth mother.

After my mother died, I looked for the books and my adoption file in the metal case where my parents kept important papers; it was a way of self-soothing, to go through these documents I had gone through as a child, but the books and the file were gone, as were my brothers'. I asked my father where they were, and he said "Oh, we threw those away when your mother and I were getting our affairs in order." My face must have registered the shock I was feeling because suddenly he looked embarrassed. "They made us sad," he said.

I nodded and walked away. I didn't want to cry in front of him and make him feel worse than he already did. I had seen in his face that he hadn't realized he'd done something wrong until that moment.

BELLYFUL OF TEARS

I started to wonder about how some babies or children might react to losing their birth mother, and how, if it did register as trauma on their systems, how that would affect the rest of their lives if it went unaddressed.

I had this feeling that my responses to certain things were not the way most people reacted. For example, when I would drive to pick up my daughter, if she left me sitting in the car for what seemed to me like too long, my body would get flooded with fury and it would take a lot of self-control not to drive off or to text her an angry message scolding her for forgetting about me. It is like this for me almost any time someone is late, and it has cost me friendships and perhaps my second marriage.

What if I react like this because there is a pattern in my brain that associates a person not showing up with abandonment, and that baby pattern in my brain is screaming *You are worthless. You are unwanted. You are going to be alone and you are going to die because no one is going to take care of you?*

I understand that this may seem insane to you, and please know that I feel insane during these times, and more often than not ashamed and teary afterwards.

I had my own bellyful of tears that had hardened into confusion and anger, but when you are busy with the day to day motions of living out your life and getting dinner on the table, stopping to question yourself seems to make as much sense as checking the engine of your car as you hurtle down the 280 to Palo Alto, attempting to keep up with the VCs in their Teslas.

However, the quality of my life was now being compromised. I didn't get a job that paid nine dollars an hour for working the front desk at a health club because I either blankly stared at the woman's face as she asked me questions or a rambled on about not being quite myself because I'd just come out of a difficult marriage. The interview was, I think, as painful for the woman as it was for me. "I'm sorry," I finally said as we stood and shook hands. "I have to interview for jobs by court order so I can get alimony."

"I thought something was wrong," the woman said and I nodded and left.

I walked out onto the sidewalk and felt two inches tall. There had been an underlying spin of anxiety that I'd been living with almost my whole life that kept slowly getting more intense, more immobilizing. Every time I went off track, dropped out of school, quit a job, got divorced, the message in my head of *things are not right and you are in big trouble* got louder and more commanding and the failure of my second marriage brought it all to a point of almost unbearable confusion and physical weakness. I could barely ride a bike. My brain and my muscles were starting to shut down.

I CAN'T STOP THINKING ABOUT YOU

I decided to stop pretending adoption wasn't an obsession. I was like a dieter who'd fallen face first into a chocolate cake. I'd grown used to the feeling that thinking about adoption was like touching a hot stove—dangerous and foolish. I didn't *have* to think about adoption. It was selfish of me, a weakness in my character that I couldn't be thankful for what I had. I could be a better person and fully accept that I had the parents that I had, the family, the life without asking questions about my past. I could forget that the flesh and blood that surrounded me wasn't the same as mine—what did it matter after all? What, really, did it affect? I could forget that I'd been born with a different name; I could forget that the roots of my life were lent to me—I could say that my grandfather had been a salesman, my great-grandfather had been a sea captain, and what did it matter if people then assumed that these stories were part of my genetic make-up? Why did I have to be so particular about DNA truth?

To help you understand, let me give you a glimpse into what conversations about adoption looks like.

The nurse asks for health history, you say you don't know, you're adopted. She writes "unknown" in the big white square. Maybe your birth mother had breast cancer. Maybe your birth father had diabetes. Who knows? You aren't privy to this information.

At a sports event, you win the mile, and a parent of a friend congratulates you, asks if your parents were runners when they were young. You shrug. "I'm adopted," you say. The parent looks surprised. "Oh," he says, smiles, pats you on the back, walks away. You came from nowhere. Your parents could have been Olympic athletes or drug addicts. You could end up anything since you have no idea what cards you were dealt. Right now you are a runner.

You're on a date, and your boyfriend has your face in his hands. He is studying you. "Do you look more like your mom's side or your dad's?" he asks. "I don't know," you say. "I'm adopted." Your date looks just like his dad. Your date's life is already set in so many ways: where he will go to college, where he will raise his family, because this is New England, and in New England history and roots are powerful, and walking in your parents, footsteps is a celebrated path to follow. "So you don't live with your real parents?" he asks. Part of you wants to tell him he is an idiot—don't your parents act like real parents? But part of you, maybe a bigger part, likes that he sees you now as different, a strange abandoned soul. You pull on the mantle of generous victim. "They are the only parents I know," you say. "They feel real to me." But you are lying, and they now feel less real to you than they did a minute earlier.

You are on a plane with your baby. "She's adorable," the woman next to you says. "What's her story?" You know what the woman means. Your daughter is half Japanese and people often assume you adopted her. It makes sense to you that even what is flesh and blood isn't seen as that. It's how life is—nothing truly is yours. But that doesn't prevent you from being mouthy. "I pushed really hard and she came out," you say. The woman looks surprised and regroups quickly. "Oh," she says. "She's really yours."

I CANNOT GET YOU CLOSE ENOUGH

I was used to having the puzzle pieces of my family never perfectly match up, so it made sense in my life that I would have a daughter that most strangers would assume I had adopted. I loved, however, when people pointed out our similarities: the nose, the smile, eventually, the height. It was like getting a gift on a day that wasn't my birthday or Christmas. I'd try to breathe and not act too excited or show that I was surprised, but it was a wonderful feeling, hearing that her nose was like mine, that we had the same biting wit.

She was both me and not me.

When she was a child and as a family we would all go to a Japanese restaurant, I was used to being the only one given a fork. One time, as a joke, she called me "Whitey," and I laughed because I hated racism, hated that she might encounter it in her life, and I loved that she was turning a little bit of it on me. But all of this helped to cement my feeling that I lived slightly removed from the rest of the world. That even the one person who had come out of my body could be taken from me, seen as not mine.

YOUR WINGS THEY OPEN

Since I never separated from my mother in a healthy manner, I didn't know how to behave with my daughter after she left for college. What does it mean to be a mother of an adult? I wanted her to know that I loved her, and love for me had to do with physical intimacy: my ability to hug her, to touch her hair, to offer to get her a sandwich, something to drink. If I was far away, how would she know I loved her?

I WILL DO SOMETHING WRONG AND YOU WILL LEAVE ME

The library was one of my favorite places when I was a kid. It was one of the few places where you could get something for nothing. The main librarian, Mrs. Fish, would sometimes let me know when the boxes of new children's books had arrived and she would let me help her unpack them.

The only thing was that I had a problem returning books. Overdue books were five cents a day, and I had a quarter for my allowance which was enough to buy a candy bar. I started putting the books I hadn't returned in the back of my closet. They made piles.

Every night I would fall asleep thinking about the books, about how disappointed my parents would be if they knew about them. Money was tight in our house and I had no idea how much returning all those books would cost. To be such a burden to my parents was unthinkable. I was there to help, not to cause problems.

One reason my mother loved me so much was because I was a good girl. She loved to touch my hair, tell me I was good, blessing me with her acceptance and love. If she saw all the books, she wouldn't even know who I was anymore. She wouldn't want me around.

Mrs. Fish wouldn't let me help her with the books any more. She would see that there was something really wrong with me. She would see that I was a sneaky girl, dark, not to be trusted.

I would lie in my bed and try to fall asleep and think about the books. Why couldn't I have returned them on time? I went to the library nearly every day. I didn't know what to do with myself. I wished I could disappear or die, but I was eight years old and I had to keep moving, had to live with the fear that any day my world was going to fall apart.

And then the library announced a fine free day. I waited until my parents were out of the house and put all my books into a red radio flyer wagon and wheeled them to the library where I shoved book after book into the metal return slot. I was free.

As I pulled the rattling wagon home I vowed to always return books on time. I was a new person. Everything was going to be okay.

Two weeks later I put an overdue book into my closet. I couldn't escape myself. I was no good, but I had to keep pretending.

THIS POOL OF MYSELF

Writing this has not been easy. I am so uncomfortable staying with my voice and my story. Sometimes I feel like I'm not even breathing when I write. I am waiting for the world to collapse because I am saying all the things I thought that had to be kept quiet. I'm not sure I would have gotten to this point without HBL. He was the one who said, yes, that voice, now you are on fire, when I sent him something that felt uncomfortably personal, small, not worthy of a reader's attention.

When my friend worked up the courage to tell her husband she was afraid he was going to leave her because she had abandonment issues, he said, "That's so stupid," and so she stopped talking about it to him. He was trying to reassure her, but she it didn't work. It's so easy to get shut down when you are a person trying to talk about adoption.

PTSD

I had first gotten interested in post-traumatic stress disorder,

PTSD, when I did a two-hour-long massage on someone who come back from serving time in Iraq. Halfway into the session he had turned from a laughing soldier to a sobbing little boy. He had cried so hard I had considered calling 911, but he rolled into a fetal position and asked me to hold his hand, so I did that, held his calloused hand until he was able to take deep breaths and lie quietly while I massaged his back. When the session was over, he came out of the room to check out and he looked ten years younger.

He hugged me and then took my face in his hands. "I love you," he said, and I looked him in the eye and said "I love you, too," but I was uncomfortable and ready for him to leave. Later he emailed me and asked if I wanted to go out. I told him that it wasn't ethical for me to date clients and that I was honored to have worked with him that day and wished him all the best in the future. There was no way I was going to work with him again.

I began to read about PTSD and I saw how common it is, not just in soldiers, but anyone who has suffered from a form of trauma, which, as defined by the American Psychological Association is *an emotional response to a terrible event like an accident, rape or natural disaster. Immediately after the event, shock and denial are typical. Longer term reactions include unpredictable emotions, flashbacks, strained relationships and even physical symptoms like headaches or nausea. While these feelings are normal, some people have difficulty moving on with their lives.* Webster's "simple" definition of trauma is *a very difficult or unpleasant experience that causes someone to have mental or emotional problems usually for a long time.*

It seems so obvious to me that adoption is rife with trauma. A woman gets pregnant, perhaps unhappily, and must then carry and give birth to a baby she cannot or will not keep. The woman risks death, as all women do, during childbirth and then hands over what most people consider a miracle to a social worker or whoever is in charge and then supposedly goes on with her life like none of this had ever happened. There is a lot of forgetting that is involved. The birth mother is asked to forget about her child because, really, how rewarding would it be to wake up each day remembering the thing that you lost?

The child is asked to forget there was a birth mother because how sad would it be to wake up every morning feeling the loss of what is not there? The parents who live with the child have to live with the fear that someday their child might have the opportunity to choose between two sets of parents, and the child might choose to return to the first.

WHAT IS GOOD ABOUT YOU?

My mother struggled to make a list of possible colleges for me because my test scores were much higher than my grades, and she wanted to find a school that was made for students who hadn't been, as she put it, properly challenged. Another way would have been to say for students who hadn't tried very hard, but my parents never directly challenged me about this, or brought me to task. There was more an underground sense of disappointment and confusion as to why I wasn't doing better.

She would type up notes to me at work on Harvard stationary and leave them on my bed with her college ideas. Communicating through notes was a way to avoid fighting, an art neither my mother nor I had perfected. We were skilled at saying an angry thing and then running from the room, so we never got very far verbally when in a state of upset. Writing things down was much more effective for both of us because we could edit out most of the anger and not have to see the other person's reaction.

We could never truly follow an argument to its end because, as anger and hurt spiraled closer and closer to the truth of the hearthurt, we would have eventually come to the fact—or I would have—that I was adopted, and there we would hit the impasse of impasses: all of this was irrelevant anyway because this wasn't even my real life. This only happened once, and even though I was only about seven, I still remember the panic and despair I felt when my mother ran from the room in tears when I reminded her that I had come from someone else.

My grades weren't good enough for most of the colleges she was listing, but my mother was working on the hope that I'd get better grades this semester and that my college essay would be amazing. It was like she was taking me shopping and getting me size six dresses when really I was a ten, but when she suggested schools I could get in, like UMass or UNH, I felt angry and insulted.

During my first appointment with the counselor, she asked me to list five of my strengths. I sat there and tried not to let my pounding heart interfere with my speech. If I'd had five strengths, I wouldn't have been in the room with her. "I'm tall," I finally said.

"Tall is good," she said. "Now how about a characteristic that you developed yourself?"

I couldn't even do the list right. If only I were a snake, I could shed the dead skin and come out new, but I was stuck as I was.

We agreed I'd come back with the list a week later.

All week I thought about the list. There was so much I wasn't. I was there, after all, because I wasn't good enough to get into Harvard where my mom worked and where my best friend was set on going. I wasn't good enough to have a boyfriend. I figured that if I didn't write the list, the woman would write it for me. I was excited to see what she would list.

But she forgot.

Recently I talked to a woman who had had the same experience with her therapist as a teenager. I asked her if she had ever written the list, and she said no. She asked me if I had written mine, and I shook my head. We agreed to write our lists end email them to each other by the next day.

This is what she sent. It was the last one, of course, that broke my heart: positive, caring, loving, sensitive, sensible, organized, creative, strong, thoughtful, and worth it.

But what really did me in what that she wrote, *I did it. That was hard.*

When she was in elementary school, two girls used to tease her, telling her that she was unwanted because she was adopted. They said there was something wrong with her and that no one wanted her. When she told me about this, her face got hard and the light inside her dimmed. Part of me wanted to think she was making it up because it sounded like a cliché, but I trusted her, and I knew I didn't want to believe her because I didn't want to think about how much it must have hurt.

I wrote my list the next morning. The thing I like most about myself is that I can get people to laugh. So I started with that: funny, and then I stood over myself like I was a movie and imagined how I would move through the day, and I described the person I saw: loving, smart, beautiful, kind, intuitive, quirky, curious, faithful, successful. The last two were the hardest to write because they weren't fully developed and required work and commitment. They required that I step into myself. I wrote them down and vowed to change my behavior.

EXTRA SPECIAL

HBL wrote to me about his thoughts on adoption: *As a parent we get the child, and that's the completing you part, but then we get the extra part, the part that makes us extra special, and that's the fantasy that we gave the child a better life. That's a fallacy, though, because who knows what the child's life would have been like if the child had stayed with the birth parents. Kids fantasize that they came from a king and queen while the parents fantasize that they came from squalor.*

There will be a portion of adoptive parents that will protect this fantasy with everything they have. They will fight the idea that adoption is traumatic because they might feel the extra special thing, the fact that they saved their children, has been taken way.

When I say my children are adopted people look as us and try to figure out who is infertile. You shooting blanks? they say. Whose fault was it? People also say, You saved that child, but I didn't save him. I was feeding my desire first and foremost. I saved me.

FLY AWAY

The day before the social worker was scheduled to come visit, my mother panicked with the sudden realization that their apartment was not up to par because she and my father didn't have curtains in the kitchen window. My mother went out and bought yards of yellow gingham. She and her sister, who had come to town from Massachusetts to help prepare for the visit, stitched up the curtains, and my mother stood up on the radiator to hang the curtains over the open window. A sharp wind swept through the kitchen and snatched them from her hands, and she wept as she watched her handiwork sail over the Hudson River. How would she ever get a baby now?

She told me this story countless times. She loved to talk about her fear, about choosing a fabric that looked like home to her. She loved describing the curtains sailing over Riverside Drive, over the Hudson River. The point of the story was twofold: I was wanted enough for this whole fiasco to have occurred and that my mother was the star of her own thrilling and disappointing world.

Years later, as an adult, I learned that when someone looks up and to the left it means she is lying, to the right it means she is remembering. Or maybe it's the other way around. Anyway, I never knew when my mother was telling the straight truth. She was happiest, I think, when she wasn't.

WHAT'S TRUE?

When people ask if I look like my mother or my father, I freeze. I look like both of them: I have their light eyes, their fair skin, their way of moving in the world, but if I said I looked like one or the other, I would feel like I was misrepresenting myself to whoever was asking. I would feel like a liar. When a person asks if you look like your parents, that person is talking about genetics, not coincidence. By answering "yes" I am disregarding the fact that, somewhere, I have birth parents whose genetics I actually carry. I am disregarding the existence of my own family tree and therefore myself, my roots; and I am misrepresenting the relationship I have with my parents. They are my parents, but they aren't my biological parents. They aren't. I'm sorry. I feel like a jerk writing this. Like, somehow, I should have done better at erasing my own history and made everyone else happy.

I'm not sure why I feel so obligated to tell the truth about myself when I have no problem lying to people about how much I eat or spend or what I do with my time. But there it is. I do.

BIG MACS COST MONEY

It is expensive to raise a child, and three children makes even a trip to McDonald's a thing to calculate. So while my parents watched the world spin and talked about what could and should be, I wondered what had possessed them to adopt three children. They could have stopped at one, had a more manageable life, but they'd shot for the dream: we had the big white house, the dog, the two cars in the driveway. Three children were part of the American dream. That made a family. We were a family. We were the Heffrons: Anne, John, and Sam: children of Margery and Frank Heffron on High Street in Westwood.

The fact that Sam had curly hair and brown eyes and brown skin and the fact that John had emotional problems because his birth mother had been a drug addict and the fact that I looked German while my parents looked like a blend of English and Irish were the *yes, but* facts of our lives: *yes*, we look different *but* we are still all related. No, not by blood. No, not *really* related, but this isn't something we talk about, you just need to play along. This is how adoption works: you acknowledge it but you also pretend that it didn't really happen. You will your way to family, to we are no different from the Maloneys across the street or the Sugrues across town. They are a father and a mother and three children: they are a family. And so are we. End of story.

But stop for a second. How can you take three children from different parents, one child adopted at ten weeks, one child adopted at eight weeks, and one child adopted at two years, and how can you expect this group of wildly different human beings to act like a normal family? You can wish, of course. You can will it through blind disregard of roots: these are my children, mine. You can stand your ground and say there is no difference between adopting a child and creating it yourself. And all of these things might be true. But they weren't for my family. And it was the pretending that we were normal that was the problem. We needed help, and we didn't get it. No one was talking about attachment disorder or PTSD or the challenge of raising an adopted child.

People really, really want to believe in the healing powers of love. They want to believe that you can take a child into your home and love away the past. And maybe you can. But I didn't see it happen in my family, despite the noble efforts of my parents and my mother's determination to pretend our lives began the day they got us.

LET ME TELL YOU

Wild love blurs the details. The wonderment of adoption is that a couple goes from paperwork to child, and the physical moment, the moment where the baby is put into the parents' arms often happens suddenly after a long waiting. There's a call, the notice that a baby is available. There is a scramble to Macy's baby section. My mother loved to talk about the bewilderment on the cashier's face when the girl asked my flat-bellied mother when the baby was due, and my mother gleefully said, "Tomorrow!"

I have never seen my mother happy in a store, but she made it sound like she went crazy in Macy's, my parsimonious mother buying a crib and bags and bags of clothing and bedding and supplies. I never asked who set up the crib or why she later told me their apartment was so small I slept in a dresser drawer.

The focus wasn't so much on *these are the facts of your childhood*. The focus was on *this makes a better story*.

THE TRUTH IS WATER

It was a wintery Saturday, and I really wanted a Snicker's bar, but they were twenty-five cents and I didn't have any money. It was my job to dust the house that morning, and in my parents' room I saw a five-dollar bill on my father's dresser. Something clicked in my brain: that five dollars could be mine if I made up a good story.

I ran out the back door and sidled around the house to the front yard and lay the five dollars on the snow. I snuck back inside to the kitchen where my parents were eating lunch. "It sure is snowy," I said, walking over to the window. "Hey! Look!" I said, "There's money out there!" I ran outside and grabbed the five-dollar bill, waved to my parents who were watching me in the window, and headed for the store. I was ten years old and had a valuable new skill.

WHAT DO YOU WANT?

HBL asked me to give him a perfect scenario for my life—the story of how it could have gone more smoothly. He was thinking of how to best parent his own adolescent boys. He was afraid to bring up the topic of adoption with them because it felt like a can of worms he wasn't prepared to handle.

I had to tell him I'd get back to him. I had no easy answer.

I remembered what my young daughter had once told me when I asked her why she didn't have tantrums in the toy store the times I didn't buy her the things she wanted. "You get what you get and you don't throw a fit," she had said. I'd immediately called her father to tell him and we laughed because she hadn't learned that from either of us.

Part of me wanted to tell HBL that the way I'd been raised was fine, that really, there was nothing that could have been done: my parents had loved me, had done their best, and for me to step and suggest alternative behaviors seemed critical and small.

But then why was I writing this book?

I think this is a common feeling for adoptees. They struggle with the way things are, but the idea of actually stepping into the spotlight and talking about their needs would be like trying to peel off their own skin.

FOR EXAMPLE

When I was a freshman in high school, I needed new underwear. I had gotten down to one pair of underpants and one bra, and I was afraid to tell my mother. I was embarrassed to talk about underwear—the word "bra" was almost impossible for me to say— and it seemed she should have known about this; she should have provided for me, but if I told her the situation, she would see that she had failed as a mother and would suffer, and so I just kept wearing dirty underwear and hoping no one ever found out.

The fact that I was adopted made this kind of thing even more complicated because I was also worried that my mother would realize that maybe she shouldn't have adopted me, that maybe the social worker should have known that my mother wouldn't be able to provide for my basic needs. I was also angry. My other friends had mothers who took them clothes shopping on a more regular basis. I was less valuable than my friends, I could see, because their parents saw their needs and met them and mine didn't always do that.

My underwear made me afraid to have a boyfriend because I would worry about what I would do if he tried to unbutton my shirt, or, more unthinkable, put his hand down my pants. It made me shy in gym class. I had to always change in the toilet stall so no one would see my dingy bra and panties.

One time I slept over my best friend's house and I when I left I forgot to take home my bag of clothes after we'd been swimming. When I realized I had left my underwear there, I raced back to her house. Her family wasn't there, but they always left the front door open and so I went in and got my bag. My underpants were right on top, unthinkably dirty. Like a street person's.

I walked home and threw the underpants into the woods between our houses. My friend never said a word. She was my best friend in the world and I was humiliated. I was dirty and there was clearly something wrong with me, but we just went on with our lives, and for a while I didn't wear underpants until finally one Saturday morning I sat next to my mom when she was sitting at the dining room table making her checklist of activities for the day, and said I had a great idea. I said that I was a little low on underwear and wouldn't it be nice if the two of us could take some time and go to TJ Maxx together. I said I was sorry about the money and that I didn't have enough of my own, but that it was something I needed.

My mother broke her day into half an hour increments and made charts of how she planned to use that time. There was no gap that day for a trip to TJ Maxx, and so I stood up, so embarrassed that I had showed need and horrified that she hadn't seen the need was real, and because I didn't know what else to do with myself, I went down into the cellar and lay my cheek against the cool metal of the washing machine and cried.

The next Saturday by some miracle my friend's mother took us to Marshall's. My mom gave me fifty dollars and I bought two pairs of underpants and a bra. I was too embarrassed to buy more as I didn't want my friend and her mother to think I was desperate, so I used the rest of the money to buy a pair of pants and a shirt.

BE QUIET

When I was a little girl, my class acted out *The Wizard of Oz* for the parents. I played Dorothy, and when the Wizard asked me what it was that I—after he had asked all the others—wanted, I looked behind me to see who was there, and the parents laughed.

"Nothing," I finally said, forgetting all that we had rehearsed.

"You want to go home," my teacher stage whispered, and I nodded. I wanted to go home. I just couldn't say it.

MIRROR IMAGE

I was a fat baby. My mother liked to say that when she was pushing my carriage around Central Park, people would stop her to count the rings of fat on my legs and neck and then tell her I should be in baby food commercials. My birth parents must have done well at sports like rugby or basketball or perhaps just sidling up to a bar while my parents were more suited for the finely-boned sports of badminton or horseshoes.

When I was almost six feet tall as a teenager, my parents had a habit of commenting on my height and size, so I began to hunch over: head forward, shoulders collapsed inward to be more like my mom and dad. I even developed an eating disorder in college and went from weighing 148 to my mother's weight of 132. It was a wonderful feeling when I went into her closet and pulled on her old Levi's and found that they fit. I was my mother's daughter, but then I ended up sinking into the 120's for a while to take the win.

I finally found peace of mind with the whole weight issue when I learned that my birth mother was 5' 10" like me and weighed 150 when she was in college. I was in my 40's when I read those facts, and you can imagine my relief. I wasn't a pig. I was my genetics.

THERE MUST BE MORE

My hunger scared me. It was bottomless. There was a thick white hook in the ceiling of my bedroom and it was a warning of where hunger could take me.

In the 1890's, two sisters, Miss Annie and Miss Lulu, had lived in our house. I know this story because my mother wrote about it for her final article as a reporter for our local paper. The article was titled *Miss Annie and Her Love of Books*. Miss Annie was the first librarian of our town, and it is documented in Westwood archives that she fiercely protected the books, scolding patrons who returned books late or damaged. I don't know what Miss Lulu did, only that one day she fell in love with a travelling salesman who had come to town, and they planned a wedding two blocks from the house at St. Margaret Mary's, but the salesman jilted Miss Lulu and she had to walk home in shame.

The story is that she got very heavy and spent the remainder of her life in a hammock that hung from the white hook. She eventually went blind and died.

This story was one reason my mother had wanted our house so badly. It was a colonial with a sagging roof and horsehair plaster in the walls—my father's nightmare—but my mother would cry every time they drove past the house until my father gave in and agreed to make an offer. She wanted the big white house with a storied past. My father wanted a split level with no story, no history, just easy plumbing, but he rarely got what he really wanted in his marriage. A type B has to expect that when he marries a type A.

If a person has died in a house, the seller has to reveal this fact to the buyer. Why? Does the death affect the structure of the walls, the strength of the floors? What does it matter if a person has died in the room where you sit? Does it matter that someone ate herself to death in the bedroom in which I grew up? Did it affect me? And though I shared Miss Annie's name, I was afraid I shared Miss Lulu's propensity for failure.

I don't know. What I can tell you is that, most of the time, I am hungry. And not just for food. I am hungry for love.

The love of my parents, my brothers, my grandparents, my uncles and aunts and cousins, my friends, my friends' parents, my neighbors wasn't enough. It didn't hit the *spot*. They didn't love *me*, they loved the shadow of me that was walking around. It was like all these arrows of love were consistently being shot my way, but none of them hit the center, none of them nailed me to my life, none of them fastened to the soul of my being. And they couldn't hit this center because it wasn't in the room. My poor husbands. It didn't matter how much they loved me. I couldn't feel it, not really, not in a way where it seemed true, real.

I understood Miss Lulu's grief because the body shock of being abandoned by my birth mother seemed comparable to being jilted at the altar. It wasn't something that I could have articulated as a child; it was more a dark sense that Miss Lulu and I had a lot in common and that I was going to be in a lot of trouble when I fell in love. I imagined that just as Miss Lulu didn't walk out of the church intact, I hadn't left the hospital intact. Both of our true beings, perhaps, had stayed behind, waiting for the dream of love to return while the ghost of ourselves that remained went back into the world and tried to feed the hunger of loss.

JUST CALL THEM

I need to look for a job. This means I need to put together a resume. This means I need to call or write to people and ask for recommendations. I needed recommendations to apply for certain writing residencies and so I didn't apply. I need to talk to people and tell them I want to teach at a university and see if anyone knows someone who knows someone who could me get a job. I need to send letters of introduction to various English department heads across the country. I've needed to do this for a year now.

When I need to make a phone call to ask about a bill or to change reservations at a restaurant or call a bookstore to see if they have something in stock, the turtle head of my courage pulls into its shell and the task becomes onerous. This means that bills often get paid late or I don't get the information I wanted. Or I stay unemployed.

How can you call a restaurant to ask them what time they open when you don't even exist?

I know this sounds ridiculous, but there it is. And the really crazy part is that I think this happens because my brain tells me *you were adopted, you came from nowhere and that makes you a nothing, so how can you possibly make this call?*

What does a nothing look like? Well, here's a copy of my original birth certificate:

For the state of New York to decide that you can't have your original birth certificate must mean something is really messed up with you. Your friends have theirs. You got one that was revised a year after your birth, with names typed in over *mother* and *father* that are, in fact your mother's and father's names, but not your birth mother's and birth father's names. You can't have those. You, for some reason, don't deserve them.

You are shaking your head. You are annoyed with me. You don't get it. I understand. These omissions should not affect my self-esteem or ability to accomplish simple tasks. But they do.

THE FATHER

It didn't occur to me for a long time that as well as having a birth mother, I had a birth father. And then I couldn't get him off my mind. From the paperwork my parents had gotten from the adoption agency I knew that, according to my birth mother, he was 6'2', blonde, 21, in good shape, and in the Navy or the Merchant Marines or some sort of maritime military. Maybe the Coast Guard. It's not something I can go check since the paperwork no longer exists.

I wish there was a DNA test where I could give a sampling of blood and a name would spit out on a white piece of paper: David Spencer (for example), along with his address and phone number.

Can you imagine? One day meeting the man who created you?

Aren't religions structured around that idea? It's a thought that I have to make small because otherwise the magnitude of the possibility, and the wave of grief that comes when I realize this will most likely not happen, makes me pass-out dizzy.

What would I give to meet my birth father? One year of my life? Absolutely. Ten years? I don't know, but I have to tell you, I would consider it. To know who my birth father was would be to know where half of me came from. It would mean I had both feet planted solidly on the ground: I would have roots that actually grew from my blood and bones.

It would be later, in New York, that I would discover a version of my dream test did in fact exist.

WORK

"I don't understand why she doesn't just get a job," my first husband said to our marriage counselor. She nodded and looked at me. My husband was almost in tears. We had a three-year-old daughter and a house with a big mortgage and he was still trying to make a financial success of his career and I spent more than I earned.

They were both being reasonable. We could put our daughter in daycare and I could get a job that paid more than the part-time teaching position I had, but the problem was I had no idea what kind of job I could get. What could I even do? I didn't have the right clothes for an office. I was tired from being a mom so I didn't even really have the energy, but moms all over the world were able to work full time and take care of their kids, so why couldn't I?

I started to cry in the office. I looked at my sweating husband, at the furrowed-browed therapist. They had no idea. They were looking at me as if I were a normal person with normal abilities, but the fact was that for someone like me, getting a job was almost impossible. I didn't have skills or confidence and I didn't have the energy or sense of self to fake it. A sense of self-worth is not always easy to see from the exterior. A person can stand tall, speak in a loud voice, and still believe in her soul that learning new things is beyond her.

YOU'RE WRONG

Being adopted can teach you that following your gut is tricky.

Your gut tells you, at birth, that something is fundamentally wrong, when really you are fine: nice people are adopting you. You are chosen. You'll have a mom. You'll have a dad. Everything will be fine. But your stomach hurts almost all the time. You think it is like this for everyone. That eating equals pain.

WHAT WOULDN'T YOU DO

In the late 1980's, I made friends with Joe Loya. If you google him now, you'll get pages of hits, but back when I knew him, he was a handsome young Mexican guy with hair slicked back to the shape of his head and a criminal record. He'd come to work as a sous chef as part of his parole at The Crocodile Café, the restaurant where I'd been waiting tables since dropping out of Occidental College.

I liked Joe immediately. He loved woman and was generous with praise and attention. He had a girlfriend, but that didn't keep him flirting with every woman on staff, including me, and he had a talent for making each woman feel that she was special.

We bonded over our love of books. We were both avid readers and had dreams of writing books of our own. Joe appreciated that I'd studied creative writing at Occidental, that I had a mother who was a writer, that I could write a sentence that was clean and expressive. I was a white girl from an upper middle class town in New England. I was a whole different species for him. I think he liked to show off that he had read more than I had, could quote The Bible, Nabokov, Hemingway, and while I scrambled to talk about theme and language, he was reciting whole passages from memory, evidence of both his intelligence and prison time well spent.

We'd exchange handwritten pages of story, encourage each other, tell each other that anything was possible, that a college drop-out and an ex-con could have a literary life, a future that didn't involve making and serving food to tables of people who didn't even know our names.

Joe's mother had died when he was young and my birth mother had given me up. These losses bonded us; we were both trying to define who we were in the wounded world the best we could. We were both criminals.

I told him about my worst crime, the money I had stolen from my mother by forging her writing on a check so I could leave for California, and he did not condemn me. He celebrated my hubris, my determination to escape. I felt there was hope for me, but I didn't know what to do with this kind of power. I'd dropped out of college, left my parents' dreams for a life like theirs behind. How was I going to live? What career would I have? Who *was* I?

"What wouldn't you do?" Joe asked me one time as we had toast and tea late one night at The Pantry, and, much to my surprise, I couldn't answer his question. It seemed that anything was possible—I'd even kill someone if he was threatening to kill me—and this was both liberating and frightening. Because I was adopted I had no idea what my genetics were, no idea if I was born for crime or honor. This kind of freedom of self-determination may sound wonderful, but bring a little kid into a toy store that is packed floor to ceiling with shiny items and tell her to pick anything she wants, but just one thing. The kid's probably going to cry. It's too much choice, too much freedom.

Eventually, the choices paralyzed me, and I decided to move back East to go back to college, back to a life like my parents', for the one I had chosen again was getting me nowhere: double shifts in a restaurant where the highlight was quick lines of cocaine in the bathroom and beers with the other waiters after work. But Joe said he would do the drive across country with me, and I was so excited to see my worlds meet: to drive up to my parents' house and to have my family and friends meet Joe, my wild Mexican man.

Joe called the night before we were to leave to tell me that something had come up and that he couldn't go. I was careful not to let him hear how disappointed I was—all I could think of to say was that I'd counted on him to pay for half the trip. I could hear him breathing. He sounded like a fat man even though he was thin. "You know that black and white poster you have in the living room I like so much?" he said. I nodded, as if he could hear, but if I'd spoken I would have cried. "Bring that to my house and I'll buy it from you."

I put the framed poster of the soldier kissing the nurse on VJ Day in my car and drove to South Pasadena. Joe met me at his front door and handed me a roll of twenties after taking the picture from me. "Drive safely, Youngster," he said to me, and he turned to go. We didn't hug or kiss. The door shut and he had my poster and I had his money.

Years and years later he would tell me that money had come from a garbage bag under his bed, but at the time I thought he'd earned it at work, not from robbing banks.

LOCKED UP

I went back home, lived with my parents, finished college. I had learned that not long after I'd left Los Angeles Joe had been arrested on the U.C.L.A. campus for robbing over thirty banks. His girlfriend was the one who had tipped off the F.B.I.

I felt that he would be in jail forever, that for someone to be in jail not once but twice meant that there was probably only trouble ahead, and I wished his mother hadn't died, wished his father hadn't beat him, wished he'd had a chance to be himself in the world, but at least I had something to write about: knowing Joe. It wasn't a book, but at least it was some pages. Writing about myself was like writing about a hole in the ground. Boring and empty. Writing about a guy who stole from others, now there was a story.

And then one day I was driving to San Jose State to teach, and I heard Joe being interviewed on KFOG about his memoir, *The Man Who Outgrew His Prison Cell*. Joe was out. And he had written a book. He had done it.

I googled him and found his email address and wrote, *You may not remember me, but we knew each other almost fifteen years ago in Los Angeles.* Almost immediately I got a return email: *I have been looking for you,* he wrote. *Can you come to my reading tomorrow night in San Francisco?*

I brought my young daughter to Books Inc. and I showed her the photograph of Joe on the cover of his book, "That's him," I said. The picture had been taken by a surveillance camera, and it showed Joe like a movie star, striding in to get his take. I picked up a copy and held in in my hand. He had done what we had talked about all those years ago. He'd written his book after seven years in prison. What was it going to take for me to break out of the prison I'd built of my life and write mine?

DON'T TALK ABOUT IT

As much as my mother had taught me to love writing, she also, unintentionally, taught me to fear it. In 1961 she was the first group of Peace Corps volunteers to go to Nigeria, and early in her stay she wrote a postcard to a friend that mentioned the "squalor and absolutely primitive living conditions" in Ibadan. The story she told was that she dropped the postcard before mailing it and some Nigerian students found it and had copies made which they then distributed and caused a near riot of angry Nigerians. My mother was sent into hiding and flown back home to United States where she was greeted by the press and my father, who pulled her aside and asked her to marry him.

My mother was deeply ashamed of the trouble she caused for both her beloved Peace Corps and her beloved President Kennedy. Although she hated to talk about her time in the Peace Corps, she did have a couple of African artifacts hanging on the walls of our house, and she also had a framed letter thanking her for her service from President Kennedy hanging over her desk. Even as a child I felt her shame was disproportional to her actions, and I tried to convince her to write about what happened, but she would always look away and ask me to change the subject.

I wanted to figure out a way to convince my mom to write the way Ole Golly had in *Harriet the Spy* after Harriet had gotten in trouble for the things she had written about her friends and schoolmates in her journal. Ole Golly had written,

I have been thinking about you and have decided that if you are ever going to become a writer it is time you get cracking. You are eleven years old and haven't written a thing but notes. Make a story out of some of those notes and send them to me. 'Beauty is truth, truth beauty—that is all Ye know on earth, and all ye need to know.' John Keats.

Now in case you ever run into the following problem, I want to tell you about it. Naturally, you put down the truth in your notebook. What would be the point if you didn't? And naturally those notebooks should not be read by anyone else, but if they are, then, Harriet, you are going to have to do two things, and you don't like either one of them:

1) You have to apologize.

2) You have to lie.

Otherwise you are going to lose a friend. Little lies that make people feel better are not bad, like thanking someone for a meal they made even if you hated it, or telling a sick person they look better when they don't, or someone with a hideous new hat that it's lovely. Remember that writing is to put love in the world, not use against your friends. But to yourself you must always tell the truth...

STICKING THE PIG

For a brief time, I lived with a boyfriend during the time I was ping-ponging from the East Coast to L.A. He drove a blue Corvette Stingray and had thinning brown hair. The one time I met his parents, his mom cried as we left the house. "She thinks you're a gold digger," my boyfriend explained in the car. I was twenty-two years old dating someone almost twice my age, and he cried as we drove away from his parents' house. "I'm sorry," he said. "She doesn't know you."

I liked him. He was so kind to me, and although I hadn't thought he was attractive the first time I'd seen him, I loved how gentle his brown eyes were and I loved his fine hands. I didn't know what love was, but I thought that maybe I loved him. He talked about what he would be like when we were married and I was pregnant. He told me he would take care of me. He asked me when I was going to get a job.

I spent many of the afternoons sitting by the pool, watching the lizard man float on his orange raft, his skin so brown it looked fake. I was waiting until I felt normal enough to go out into the world and get some work. I was so off track I had no idea what to do next. The last time I'd decided L.A. wasn't for me anymore and driven back to the East Coast, I'd turned around after a week and come right back. I figured I'd have to go and get another waitressing job, but just the thought of folding another napkin made me exhausted. So I was waiting day after day by the pool until I had the confidence to try something different. My boyfriend knew there was something wrong because I cried about not working and about feeling lost in my life, but he wasn't giving me money and I barely had any of my own, so something was going to have to change soon.

He wanted to take me to Wolfgang Puck's new restaurant, but I had no nice clothes. When he was at his restaurant, I took his nearly life-sized Mexican porcelain piggy bank and lay on the floor with it by my side. I was on my back and I bent my legs like I was going to play airplane with a child, and I put the pig, slit side down, on my shins. I had found a barbeque skewer in the kitchen, and I slowly skewered the pig there in the living room. I was able to hook bill after bill with the metal edge and gently ease the bills out of the slit. The money rained down on me, and after a little work, I had two hundred and sixty dollars in twenties, tens, and fives. I put the pig back in the corner of the room and went to Bullock's to buy a dress that was flowered and pretty.

On the bathroom mirror he'd taped a photograph of a picture he'd taken of me with a yellow stickie on top where he'd scrawled, "I can't believe you like me"—something I had said to him on our first date when, drunk, I'd pulled away from his grasp and looked into his sad eyes.

When I emptied his wallet a month later early one morning and drove across the country to go back to school, he threw all my things into a cardboard box and mailed it to me. I unpacked it in my parents' basement and dried rose petals fell to the floor. I'd bought him a ceramic fruit bowl, and he'd thrown that into the box as well. I shook the pieces and shards out of the clothes I'd left behind.

I'd left that morning because the two weeks had passed since I'd started taking birth control, and we were finally going to have sex for the first time that day. No one believes me when I tell them that I was terrified of sex at twenty-two, but I was. I'd had had sex before— but not with anyone I lived with. Not with anyone I couldn't escape from almost immediately afterwards. I wanted to do it; I wanted to stay, but I couldn't. It was too much. I needed to escape before he really saw me.

WATCH OUT

A recklessness comes with adoption. If I wasn't good enough to keep, then anything is possible. I can do anything, find once unthinkable new lows in the search for the true nature of my being.

DON'T TAKE IT FOR GRANTED

The bubble of thought in an adopted person's mind when the teacher says *Today we will draw a family tree*: (how?).

TIGHT

It wasn't until she was dying from cancer that some Peace Corps volunteers from her class convinced her to go to their 50th reunion, and my mother came back shaken by their acceptance and love. After she died, I did a little research and contacted some of the

126

people who had been in Nigeria with her, and the story I got was different from the story my mother had told me. The man who had been her supervisor at the time told me that the most likely scenario was that the Nigerian students had stolen the postcard and that my mother had been a sacrificial lamb for the student's anger about the United States' arrogance in coming to Nigeria. None of these people understood why my mother had been so ashamed of the event. *Anyone of us could have written what she did,* her supervisor said. *It wasn't her fault.*

I always wondered what my mother's adult life would have been like if she had removed the mantle of shame she wore and turned it into a book instead, one that talked about the first wave of Peace Corps volunteers and what actually happened when two cultures, Nigerian and American, came together. I wonder if it would have helped me to feel that writing about adoption would have been okay, that instead of internalizing shame and guilt I would have seen that it was okay to process those feelings and to turn them into strengths.

With my work teaching writing in the girls' juvenile hall and from talking with friends and from doing massage in a pain clinic, I have seen that it's the stories we don't tell that keep us in various states of paralysis. Think back to when you were a little kid, and someone told you a secret. Your job was to keep it inside and not tell anyone. Think about how, physically, you had to tighten areas of your body—your stomach maybe, your throat, your face. Maybe even your hands. People store secrets in the funniest places. The space between their shoulder blades. Their lower back. Their heart.

Think of people coming out of confession, for example. There are often tears, shaking, an overall softening. The body knows what is true, and the diaphragm and guts move more freely when we lay down our painful stories.

I wonder where the Peace Corps story was stored in my mother's body. I wonder where the story of letting me go was stored in my birth mother's body. I wonder where the story that I was not wanted by my birth mother is stored in my body. The last time I went to a new chiropractor I wrote "my skin is too tight" on the intake form. So maybe the story is systemic—a skin straight jacket.

When I get a massage, I am so used to the therapist saying "Oh" every time she gets to a new area. "I know," I say. "I'm tight." I'm told to stretch, to drink more water, but mostly I'm told to relax. If I could relax, I would. I've been doing yoga for seventeen years. I meditate. I am a massage therapist. I am the queen of trying to relax.

It's easy not to talk about adoption. I you don't mention it, everything is fine, but once you say "I was thinking about my adoption" to your parents when they ask you what's on your mind over dinner, for example, for many families, a new tension walks into the room, and as the child prays for an open door of free speech and total acceptance of self, the parent prays for the conversation to end. Everyone stiffens.

I know there are plenty of parents who have absolutely no problem talking about adoption with their children, but they weren't my parents—my mother in particular; my father was much more at ease with the topic—and they aren't the parents of many, many adopted kids. And it's not the parents' fault. What parent truly wants to acknowledge that their child, whom they love more than life itself, actually has a birth mother out there somewhere, a birth father, who, god only knows, could appear out of nowhere and demand, without regard to legal recourse, the return of their child—their flesh and blood, which is not your flesh and blood, no matter how many diapers you changed, no matter how fully you handed over your heart.

I can't think of anything with which to compare saying "I'm

adopted" to mostly because it's not clear if it is a positively or negatively charged statement. You say it and often there is a beat as the other person tries to read your face, tries to figure out what to say.

The poet Keats wrote about negative capability, which he defined as *the ability to contemplate the world without the desire to try and reconcile contradictory aspects or fit it into closed and rational systems.*

Part of my brain is always trying to puzzle out the fact that I am Anne Heffron and that I am also a ghost person—the person on my original birth certificate. It's not a name I can say to a larger audience because there are people related to my birth mother who don't know about me—her husband for example. This thought makes my neck go stiff as I type. The fact that I need to hide aspects of myself because of another person's shame affects not only the freedom I have to talk about myself, but it also affects the free movement of my body.

HELLO, DADDY

I drove two hours to Marin in order to see a biodynamic

craniosacral practitioner. I had never had this kind of work done, but I'd listened to a podcast in which this man was mentioned and was interested to see what a session would be like.

I lay on the table, fully clothed, and the gentle-eyed man asked if I could feel the skin on my toes. I was so in my head it took a while for me to feel those little casings, and finally, though I didn't exactly feel the skin, at least I had an awareness there was something at the end of my feet. Then he asked if I could feel the skin on top of my feet, on the bottom, and as I nodded, he worked his way up slowly to the skin on my head. By the time he was finished, I was a bag of skin. This was a new feeling, and I took a deep breath and let the skin expand until I was nothing but space.

Then he asked me if I could feel the bones in my toes. I opened my eyes and stared at the ceiling. After all those years of studying anatomy I had never really stopped to consider that each of the 206 bones I had learned the names of resided in me. That I was tarsals, metatarsals, phalanges. That I was calcium and collagen. That I was an actual skeleton reclining on the table. That I carried my final coffin within me.

I imagined the bones: the navicular, the tibia, the femur, the ilium, the wild line of vertebra, the clavicle, the humerus, the carpals, the maxilla, the occipital. I had never felt so present in my life. I lay on his table and cried. I was real.

Then things started getting weird. He sat next to me with one hand on my shoulder and the other on my hip. I had the floaty, sweet feeling I'd get in yoga class lying in savasana. My face started to shift. It was like I was photo shopping myself, the bones and skin reorganizing into someone else. I became my birth father; someone I had never seen. Someone whose name I didn't know. I waited for the man to say something to me, like, *Hey, what's going on with your face?* but he kept slowing breathing and so I did the same, feeling the heavy maleness of this strange face on what was once my face. I breathed and waited to see what would happen next.

What happened next is that I became a gun.

You can see why this isn't a story I walk around and tell people.

My face and body filled with steel and I felt the anger and cold heft of metal. I thought about how when Antonia and I were writing *Phantom Halo* we went nuts when we brought a gun into the third act. We shot almost everyone in the room. One critic said later that we were two women trying to write like men. I thought about anger as I lay on the table as a gun. I thought about the fact that it was part of who I was at the moment, and that it was just a feeling, not anything I had to fear.

Soon I was no longer my birth father, no longer a gun. I was myself, skin and bones and the organs and tissues that kept me alive and warm. I wanted to Xerox myself so I could remember this feeling forever. This space of vital acceptance was where I wanted to live. In my body.

I had to figure out what to do with all the stories I carried in my head, the stories that told me who I was and how to think and feel.

CURIOUS

A powerful response when someone tells you he or she is adopted is "And what has that experience been like for you?" Perhaps the relief of telling story will allow the body to soften, will allow the teller to exist more easily in his or her skin.

WHAT WILL I LOOK LIKE LATER?

My daughter has bunions, and we know where they came from because her grandmother, her father's mother, has the same knobbed feet. There is solace in the history of the body even if it is bad news: at least you know you are not alone, that this malady is part of being one of the Jones.

For a long time, I had no idea what to expect as far as my body goes, and when I found my birth mother's family and was told that breast cancer wasn't a scare, for example, I felt relief. One time I had a phone conversation with my birth mother's brother, and it was sweet. We laughed over the fact that we both farted when we ate bread. I don't know how we got to that topic, but we did, and it made the farting better. *This runs in the family*, I thought afterward as I let one fly after eating a turkey sandwich. It wasn't all my fault.

FISH

All those years ago, the captain had come up to me on the boat, whispered *kiss me* right in front of my young daughter, in front of all the other fishermen. He'd caught a huge haddock while everyone else was tugging on empty lines, and he'd dropped that fish into my bucket and, somehow, because he had given me a fish, I was his.

He was blonde and handsome and funny and rude. If I had been a man, I would have been the captain. I hoped my birth father was someone like the captain: a rule breaker, a heart breaker, the catcher of fish.

We had sex in the parking lot of a Mexican restaurant that night. He'd told his wife he'd forgotten something on the boat, and I asked my parents to watch my daughter so that I could run to the drugstore. We didn't kiss. He smelled like Clorox and lemons and every summer I'd take my daughter fishing on the boat, and every summer the captain and I would meet in parking lots—once a motel— and have quick sex and then he would take me for a drive in his truck to get iced coffee at Dunkin' Donuts and show me different parts of the shore. One time he was narrating what we were passing: *This is where my son plays baseball, this is where the dwarfs live, and that's my mother-in-law.* He pulled the handle on my car seat and suddenly I was reclining, facing the ceiling.

I was so happy. Whenever I went on the boat, one of the mates would walk by and hand me the captain's rod, which was a serious piece of fishing business. It had his name on it, in script, embossed in gold. Everyone else used the beat up yellow ones that caught when you tried to reel in a fish. The captain would walk past me while I fished and pretend I wasn't there, and I would smile and hope for a keeper.

This was the truest relationship with a man I'd ever had—I got to feel worthless and valuable at the same time. I was someone who needed to be kept secret, someone to hide. I liked that he was married, that there was no pressure to actually talk to him or get to know each other. I had nothing to say to him, and it was a relief to not have to fake intimacy.

My junior year in high school, we had a Sadie Hawkins dance, and I decided to ask Ricky Canin. He was a year older than I was and ran the quarter mile on the track team. I loved his laugh and was scared of him because he was either a little shy or mean, I couldn't tell which. We had never talked before, but I wanted to get to know him and I thought this dance would be the perfect way to his heart.

The days were slipping by, and finally I approached him by the water fountain in the cafeteria. He looked up at me, wiped his mouth, and started to walk away. "Don't do it," he said. I was surprised into humor.

"Are you kidding? Why?"

He walked faster. "It's not a good idea."

I walked faster, too. "How do you know?"

He started running. "I just do," he said, and he pushed through the double doors and ran to the science wing. I stood there thinking about how to frame what just happened to my friends. People told me I was pretty. They told me I was special. Funny. Smart. Then why didn't boys like me? Why was it that when we had gone to the roller dance club on Kenmore that all of my friends had boys ask them to skate and no one asked me?

I told my friends that he had said someone else had asked him and asked Paul Giametti instead. He was quiet and strange and I knew he would say yes because I'd seen him staring at me in the halls. There was something busted inside of him, too.

HUSH

My mother loved words, and she loved to talk. She called me Constant Comment in an effort to get me to talk less so she could talk more.

My mother loved me most, I think, when I was curled up in a chair reading, for it was then that I was the clearest reflection she had of herself.

When my parents had adopted me as an infant, they assumed they were getting someone who would be like them: smart, moral, liberal, an overall decent human being, and that's what I tried to become.

I loved my father, but that was like loving the tree in front of my house: neither was going anywhere. I loved my mother differently. She was mercurial, needy, but so was I.

I was angry at her much of the time. She liked to present herself to the world as a working mother who was capable of doing it all, but her actions confused me. She'd read her *Ms. Magazine* hungrily, quoting articles that talked about how women could have or be anything, but then she'd groan at her own reflection in the mirror, slapping it. She'd teach me how to say *ou se trouvent les toilettes* as if

138

we were going to Paris the next week, as if she'd been there herself, but she'd have stains on her shirt and she'd anxiously parse out our allowances every Friday.

I wanted her to see that she really was a queen, that France was a possibility for her, that anything was possible if she stopped using the word "grim" so much. I wanted her to look into the mirror and love her reflection instead of turning away.

It didn't matter how much she praised me when I could see that the beliefs she had about herself were critical and unkind. How could I be any good if, in her secret heart of hearts, she didn't think she was? This also made me, deep down, furious. How could I be special, if my mother wasn't? I felt fundamentally gypped that I'd been adopted by someone who wasn't saying that anything was possible, that I could be whoever I wanted. I recognized that I was there to mirror my mother, but not outshine.

THE QUEEN WILL RETURN

One time when I was a little girl, my mother asked me to sweep the floor and I told her that my real mother, the queen, was

139

going to be very angry when she came back to get me and heard how I had been treated. I imagined my birth mother was like the ice queen in *The Lion, The Witch, and the Wardrobe*, beautiful, robed in white fur. My mother hadn't argued with me or tried to explain that no one was ever coming to get me: instead, she burst into tears and ran from the room.

I was horrified and conflicted. My mother had run from me. I saw how bad I was, how dangerous. I was a little girl who wasn't good enough for one mother to keep and who could hurt the next so badly she had to run.

HOLES

I'd long lost track of how many needles my acupuncturist Nora had stuck in me. They were in my skull, my jaw, my forearms, my lower legs, and my feet. After a little while it was like my skin had disappeared and I was a soul and a pair of eyes. Every once in a while Nora would stand at an angle from me, pushing her hand over my abdomen like a movie star turning from the paparazzi. When her hand swept over my solar plexus, cold air blew on my skin. I asked her what she was doing.

"Creating holes in the space between us. Our energies are separate, there is your energy and my energy, and in the space between I look for heaviness, and I even it out. Then I make holes so the heaviness can escape. We are all one. There is no separation. That's where the freedom is."

STAY UP ALL NIGHT

The first semester of graduate school, our teacher told us that his teacher, Donald Barthelme, had told him to stay up all night and write as a way to break through writer's block. We didn't necessarily have writer's block, but we liked the idea of staying up all night, so Erdäg, Ryan and I decided to make an event out of it. We drove to the Oregon coast and got a motel room for the night and plugged in our computers and got to work.

At one point the motel manager banged on the door. Apparently a neighbor had complained about the noise we were making. The manager was surprised to see our computers, our bags of Doritos and bottles of Diet Coke. No drugs. No alcohol. "We're writers," Erdäg explained. The manager looked us over: two men, one woman, one motel room. "Not sure why you had to come here to do this," he said.

"We're trying to get out of our heads," Erdäg said.

"Well do it more quietly," the manager said, and we agreed that we would.

An hour later we were out in the near dark, looking out over the ocean as a lighthouse flashed its warning. The wind was blowing my hair and my skirt as I stood in the middle of the grassy area and closed my eyes, feeling, listening, trying to remember everything. Being a writer was amazing.

"You look like you are longing for something," Ryan said. I hadn't known he was there. I thought he and Erdäg were still trying to scale the lighthouse.

I liked that Ryan had seen longing in me. I hadn't realized it until he said it, but I was always longing for something. Longing in my body was so familiar I didn't usually notice the feeling; that would have been like a magnet experiencing its own field, the pull toward, the hungry mouth.

It was easy to mistake the emptiness of longing as something that wanted filling with M&M's, time with friends, new clothes, accomplishments, a boyfriend, and it was also easy to be frightened by the ceaseless dark cave call *of I am alone and I may die*. I thought it meant something that Ryan saw this longing in me. I thought it meant that maybe I wasn't alone.

Two years later, Ryan and I got married.

Four years later we had a baby.

Seven years later we got divorced.

The closer people tried to get to me, the more problematic longing became. Aside from my daughter, I wanted anything but who or what was right in front of me. The best thing about being married was that I could project all of my problems onto my husband instead of having to look inside and face the fact that the emptiness I'd been carrying for so long was taking over.

SNOT

More than ten years later, I took an autobiography class with my friend at The Grotto in San Francisco, mostly because I figured

I'd be so much better than the other rookie writers in the class, and I needed an ego boost from the pits of my second marriage. I wrote about being friends with a bank robber, and when the day came for me to hand in my five pages for workshop, the class and the teacher agreed that I had wonderful dialogue, but that the character need wasn't clear.

I cried so hard in class there were tears and snot running down my face into my turtleneck. I'd heard exactly the same thing so long ago in graduate school. As a writer and as a human being I had not grown at all.

I had first heard about character need back when I was an undergraduate. I had no idea what my teacher there was talking about, so I asked my boyfriend who was getting his PhD in creative writing. He tried to explain and I listened carefully. "I think what my character needs is a hug," I finally said, proud to have broken through this tricky concept. How can you name a person's driving need, after all? We each have so many.

My boyfriend guffawed. "A hug! That's not a need."

I was flabbergasted. I had revealed something deep and true about myself: more than anything I needed to be held, but apparently this didn't add up to anything meaningful. I didn't understand why my boyfriend who was so good at analyzing texts couldn't recognize the depth of my insight. Nights I couldn't sleep I would imagine someone warm and bearded, Jesus maybe, spooning me, warming my back with the heat of his body, letting me know that everything was going to be alright, that I was not alone, that I had not been forsaken. How can you get any needier than that?

"You can do better," my boyfriend said, but I thought he was wrong. I thought I had done my very best.

For the next twenty years, I stayed on the surface and ignored character need. What I mean is, I tried to do what I thought was right: I got a job, got married, had a child, cooked dinners, bought bags full of stuff at Target. I stayed at 148 pounds. I whitened my teeth. I changed the sheets weekly, brought the car in for regular service. I was *trying.*

I cried so hard in the memoir class there were tears and snot running down my face into my turtleneck. "Oh my god," I sobbed. "I have to write about my mother."

That night I went home, and, instead of starting with my mom's name, for the first time I googled my birth mother, and what came up was her face. I had never seen her as an adult. All the pretty I'd seen in her high school portrait was gone. Her face was both red and pale. She was smiling, but she didn't look happy. Her hair was reddish and looked accidentally parted down the middle. She looked like a falsely cheerful Irish cleaning lady who was pretending to happily greet you but was silently seething that you never flush the toilet.

Her picture was part of her obituary, dated two weeks earlier. After a long illness, the obituary said, she had died of lymphoma. What also came up was a list of her children, and their names. She had two sons, it was true, but she also had a daughter whose name was almost identical to mine. Anna.

I was thrilled. I had a sister. I grew up with brothers, but a sister was a thing of dreams, and one who nearly shared my name brought it close to fairy tale status. I couldn't wait to find her.

But first I googled whether lymphoma was genetic. If the answer had been yes, I would have been, as I used to say when I lived in Boston, *pissed*.

COINCIDENCES

I was the only massage therapist in a roomful of physical therapist. We were there to study Strain/Counterstrain. I was in way over my head, but I wanted to learn.

Years later I would find out that my birth mother was a physical therapist. My mom was a writer. It was like I didn't even have a choice about my careers.

When I met my half-sister I saw that she had a star tattooed on the inside of her left wrist. I pointed to the "love" tattoo I had on my left wrist. "I got this when my mom died," I said. "Me, too," she replied.

When my half-brother came to visit, we sat down and talked. At one point my husband bumped my arm and pointed to my half-brother who was thinking, his hand a cage for his face, his forefinger supporting his forehead, his index and middle finger on either cheek. "He does that thing, too!" my husband said. We laughed. My half-brother and I imitated each other being ourselves being each other.

Dec 10, 1964 I was born.

Dec 11, 2010 my birth mother's funeral.

Dec 9, 2011 my mother died.

OCEAN ADOPTION

Imagine that two dolphins got together at a beach party, a male and a female, and they had a good time, and ten or so months later the female pushed out a baby. Imagine the dolphin mother had too much on her plate to take care of a new baby, and so she gave her baby to a lovely tuna couple. The baby dolphin would be hungry and uncertain so it would quickly bond with the mother tuna for food and protection, but the baby dolphin's brain would be on high alert because nothing in the womb had prepared it to be a tuna. All its gestation period it had smelled, touched, heard, and tasted dolphin. Now everything was tuna.

Imagine the tunas had been longing for a baby of their own; the sudden appearance of the baby dolphin would seem like a gift from Poseidon. The unstated agreement between all would be *don't talk about it*.

The dolphin mother wouldn't want to say anything in

fear of being judged by others for being sexually active and for giving up her child. The baby dolphin wouldn't want to say anything because if she pointed out that she wasn't a tuna and her tuna mother might suddenly disappear, taking with her life-preserving food and safety. And what would happen if the tunas pointed out that there is actually a difference between mammals and fish? The delicate structure of *we are a family* would crumble, and the tuna parents would fear the dolphin baby might decide that she wanted to go back and find her dolphin roots, abandoning her tuna parents in her excitement of original home.

Here's the thing: these creatures would have suffered less long-term if they'd had a series of discussions. Granted, these discussions might have been painful and scary and sad, but it would be like lancing a wound.

If the birth mother had written a water-proof letter, for example, to her child, explaining why she had to let go of her little dolphin, asking for forgiveness if that was what she needed or stating her love, if that was what she wanted to say, then she could have at least felt she left something beside her child behind. If the tuna parents said they feared the dolphin mother might come back some day to reclaim her baby, the dolphin baby would feel loved and valuable. If the dolphin baby said it was strange growing up with people who looked like tunas and that she had an ache of missing in her gut for her birth mother, but that she loved her tuna parents very much, maybe there could be a happily ever after.

KEEP MOVING

I started running when I was twelve, and found relief in the movement of the road under my feet. It didn't matter who I was as long as I was moving. Later I would find other ways to run: driving, dropping out of schools, dating men, quitting jobs, packing up to live somewhere new, drinking caffeine, eating. I would have been a great alcoholic if alcohol didn't put me to sleep. I would have been a great drug addict if I liked that kind of high.

FOUR IN ONE

I was four people jammed into one: I was the me that my mom wanted; I was the me I would have been if my birth mom had kept me; I was the me I would have been if another family had adopted me; and I was the me that was just *me*. I couldn't commit to one, and so I was a little bit of all four, and this made me unpredictable and unknowable both to those around me and to myself.

ATTACHMENT DISORDER

I don't know if I can count the number of times I have left home only to return in tears. It wasn't until I started researching the effects of adoption that I finally read about attachment disorder.

I was ten the first time I went to sleepover camp. I made it a day before I started feeling sick. I told my camp leader that I wasn't feeling well and she sent me to the nurse. I told her my stomach hurt, and she had me lie down with a hot water bottle on my stomach. I liked the nurse, and, afraid the pain might suddenly leave forcing me to go back into the unknown world of the camp, I focused on making my stomach hurt more. The nurse made me hot tea and I felt safe.

It was peaceful in the nurse's room, and I didn't have to face all the kids I didn't know, the bed that wasn't really mine. The strange food. The red Kool-Aid that at camp was called bug juice. It was hard to know what the right thing to do was when the rules weren't clear— the people were new to me and I wasn't sure how I fit in to the group.

When I was home, I wanted to get away. When I was at camp, I forgot how sad my family made me. I wanted to be home. I wanted the familiar smells, the people who knew me. The very things that felt constraining when I was there seemed like a life raft when I was away at a place where people didn't know that I was special. They didn't know that I was my mother's daughter and that although I looked like the girl next door, there was something about me that my parents— my mother in particular—saw that set me apart from everyone else.

As parents, we play peek-a-boo with babies, in part, to teach them that we come back after we disappear. I think many adoptees would benefit from extended sessions of some form of peek-a-boo, perhaps even well into adulthood. The trauma of the disappearing birth mother is deep and tenacious. Adoptees need to learn that it's okay to separate from their parents. What I learned when my dad came to pick me up at camp after the third day was that I could not survive on my own, and so for years and years I would try to go away only to return, unable to bear the separation.

I think if my father would have refused to come get me that first time, I would have been terrified and desperate for escape, but time would have passed and someone would have made me laugh or asked to be my friend, and I would have slowly pulled on the suit that is the world and seen that, although it did not feel entirely comfortable, I could move around in it. I could become my own person. I could be separate from my parents and survive.

Becoming your own person sounds like a wonderful thing, and it did to me, too. But overshadowing that desire is a greater fear of separation. The fear that becoming your own person equals losing your parents equals losing safety equals dying. I think this is the glitch in the brain many adopted children have that the world at large doesn't understand. It happens quickly and it doesn't get talked about, but it is there. Remember, the moment the baby is born, everything he knew for over nine months disappears suddenly. This baby has a preverbal thinking mind, and I believe it stores this sensory memory, and some people— I don't know why it affects some people more than others—spend the rest of their lives waiting for the other shoe to drop, for the world as they know it to disappear yet again, and so they develop all sorts of defense mechanisms to prevent this from happening. The inability to attach in a healthy manner to another human being is a popular one. I've basically perfected it and have therefore spent my adult life pushing love away as vigorously as I have searched for it.

While I was at camp, I would have fought to go home if my parents had refused the nurse's suggestion that they come get me. I would have lied, faked near death, whatever I thought it would take to get them to rescue me. Any normal parent would give in, would think the child clearly needed rescue when what the child needs is a sort of inoculation to the thing she fears most: abandonment.

I LOVE YOU WHEN YOU'RE QUIET

It meant the world to my mother I loved books, loved being read to, loved reading. She had named me after Jane Austen's character Anne in *Pride and Prejudice*, and she hoped for me the traits visible in Austin's Anne: humility, intelligence, steadiness of character. Anne was not flashy. She dressed simply and lived to serve others.

My mother's insistence there was only the quiet, bookish Anne, and my need to be seen differently made me both angry and ashamed. I was afraid if my mother didn't see me, a me that I felt was truly me, I wouldn't actually exist. I was also afraid there was something wrong with me, something dirty, in my attempts to differentiate myself from my mother. Why couldn't I be who she wanted me to be? What was so wrong with quiet Anne, anyway? Why did I have to have so many needs that infringed on the ease of my mother's life?

The tensions between my mother and me became worse when she diagnosed with breast cancer weeks after I'd come back to live with them to finish college. Her eyes were a light blue that appeared bleached, like they were trying to disappear, and she would look at me as if she were drowning. Sometimes I would turn away from the pull, afraid she would drag me down with her, but I had nowhere to go. I'd gotten myself into trouble out in the world, and I had come back home, again, to be rescued, but it wasn't easy. My mother needed rescuing more.

My turning away was awful. My mother would seek me out for solace, for an ear in which to spill her fears and grief, and sometimes I would claim I had homework, claim I had a friend to visit, and could I borrow her car to go? My mother would always say it was fine, would always react as if my behavior was acceptable, that of course she was not worthy of my time. I would make myself hard in the face of her hurt, but my heart would suffer, and my head would tell me there was something seriously wrong with me, that I was a terrible person, and yet I would still leave because part of me hated her and part of me was afraid of getting too close to so much pain.

My mother's insistence on using the word *grim* to describe so much of her world made me furious. As far as I could see, even with cancer, she was capable of great happiness. She was happy in her garden, happy when she was making bread or cookies. She was happy when she was at her sewing machine, when she was reading the Sunday *New York Times*. She was happy when her friends came over and they sat around talking in loud voices and laughing. She was happy when I walked into the room.

I didn't understand her decisions. If her job left her exhausted and she wished she could write full time, why didn't she sell the house and move into an apartment? If she had to have chemotherapy, why wouldn't she take time off work so she could throw up in the privacy of her own house? My father could have stepped up to the plate—he could have been the man of the house, but my mother was so hell bent on being a *successful woman* that she wasn't going to give him the chance—she was going to be the woman and the man of the house, even when her hair was falling out, even when she was crying as she drove to work.

The worst part was she had adopted me to make her life better, and I had failed. I'd been a mistake for my birth mother and now I was a mistake for my mother.

THERAPISTS NEED TRAINING ABOUT ADOPTION

For all those years I was searching for a path to walk, why did therapists keep dismissing my suggestion that adoption was affecting me negatively? Why did so many—almost all—say, "But good people adopted you, right?" Why were people so reluctant to admit that maybe love isn't enough to heal all when it comes to adoption? That maybe the initial abandonment trauma will be with the person for his or her whole life, and what I have found by writing this book is that accepting the fact already eases so much pressure and tension. If you can talk about the monster under the bed, look at it, it's not so bad. Loss and grief are really only unbearable when they are repressed. Otherwise, they're just feelings.

I suspect that if you wake up sad, and your partner says, "What's wrong?" and you say, "I woke up thinking about my adoption and it made me sad," and your partner hugs and holds you and lets you feel loved, you will probably have an easier time of it then if you wake up feeling sad and think there is something wrong with you for feeling sad when you have a perfectly nice life. You internally scold yourself for being so difficult, and you feel a sense of dark pull of dread that this sadness inside may never leave, may take over everything.

ONE LETTER OFF

When I read stories about adoptees searching for their birth parents, worse case scenarios are presented as those when the birth mother refuses contact. These are often cited as adoptees' nightmares come true. But this happened to me, and it didn't feel like a nightmare. I had grown up with a sense of rejection, so it certainly didn't come as a big surprise.

PAY ATTENTION

My mother finally started to write a book in her sixties. She was happier than I'd ever seen her, and then she got pancreatic cancer. She wrote through the cancer, through the radiation, through chemotherapy. In the end, she wrote through morphine, although my father would try to distract her and get her away from the computer because she was starting to do more damage than good at the keyboard. And then she died and the book was not finished.

About a year later, Yale University Press published it and it was written up on the front page of *The New York Times Book Review* and in *The New Yorker*. But here's the thing: even without knowing it would be published and so favorably received, my mother still had great success with her book because she was living out her purpose, her dream. She'd had said she wanted to write a book, not to have written a book, and that's what she got: she got to write a book.

I needed to pay attention to that lesson. It was the doing that was important: not the success at the end. I was so busy trying to prove that I was a good person I was missing the experience of being myself.

HAPPY BIRTHDAY

My brother's birth mother brought him to the adoption agency right before closing time on his second birthday. As my own child got closer and closer to two, I would look at her in the rear view mirror as I drove and I would torture myself, asking, what about now? I was so afraid of what I was capable of doing—I'd already given away so much.

I would think about the physical act of abandonment. It was a series of motions, and that's what scared me. It's a series of motions. What if you did them because you could? What separates the people who can do this series of motions from the people who can't? How do you know which side of people you are on? If someone abandoned you, does that mean you are hardwired for abandonment, that it will be easier for you to leave things and people than for others? It seemed that way for me. It seemed I could leave homes, jobs, schools, and people much more easily than my friends could. I used to think the ability to walk away was my greatest strength, but I was learning it was really my greatest weakness. And yet I couldn't seem to stop.

I imagined my brother's birth mother driving to the adoption agency, hoping her car didn't break down again. I saw her taking my brother from her car seat, his arms and body sticky from the heat. I saw her kissing him on his head. Smelling his hair and humming a tuneless song to soothe him. Maybe he was getting too big to carry easily, and so she had to shift him from one side to the other. Maybe he grabbed a fistful of her shirt because she was walking so fast. "Mama," I imagine him saying. Maybe she tried not to look, but she did, and she saw his eyes, dark like hers. Maybe she saw his mouth, his teeth—white pearls. Maybe she got light-headed and thought she might pass out, and then she thought about the fact that she had no money to buy this child food and she got hard inside because her own belly was empty and she had no idea when her next meal would be. Maybe she felt angry that this child had so many needs she could not meet no matter how hard she tried. Maybe she wondered why God let her have a baby when she was eighteen years old if he wasn't also going to help her provide for it. Maybe she hated God. Hated the needs of her child. Hated herself for being weak.

Maybe she went inside. Said hello. The child's hand grabbed onto her shirt more tightly because he could feel his mother's grip loosening.

"I was here the other day," she might have said. "I filled out the paperwork." Maybe her eyes filled with tears and her mouth filled with spit and she thought she would die if she said another word. Maybe this was not going the way she had planned, but she walked around the desk and tried to hand the child over to the older woman sitting there. Maybe the child had a tight hold on her shirt, so she grabbed his little strong hand and yanked free. "Mama will be right back," she might have said to her child, which was not what she meant to say. Maybe he started crying because his mother was headed for the door. The woman holding her child started to stand up, started asking questions, but she didn't hear them because she was already out the door. She gone from inside the room to where she was still the mother to her child to outside of the building where she was not the

162

mother any more. It made no sense, how easy it was. She had gone through a door. She should have had to walk through fire.

Maybe her legs weren't working right, but somehow she was able to get to her car which she had left unlocked and running so she could drive away before anyone had time to try to catch her. Maybe she could still feel her child's hand pulling on her shirt. Maybe something merciful happened in that moment, maybe the ghost of her heart left her body, slipped out, taking most of her love with it, and maybe she could keep driving because the shell of who she was remembered how to steer.

And then what? Maybe she went back to her apartment, opened the door, lay down on the couch, listened to the silence. Maybe she put her hands over her empty belly and went to sleep. Maybe it was like her baby had never even been there. Maybe it was like she had left too much of herself behind, and she'd never be whole again. But right now, it was peaceful, like the moment when she had walked up to her mother's coffin and looked at her pale face. The whole world went silent in the gaping yawn of loss.

REAL

Language makes talking about adoption difficult. But I am going to try because I want people to understand what it is like to be adopted, and to, ideally, never again say to people like me, "Oh, you're adopted? So your parents aren't your real parents?" because as soon as you ask me that, my whole world disappears, if only for a nanosecond. And it doesn't matter how many times I have heard that question, how many times I have answered it. My brain goes through the same routine: If my parents aren't my real parents, then my brothers aren't my real brothers, my house isn't my real house, my friends aren't my real friends, and, so, ultimately, my life isn't my real life either, and, like that, I become a ghost.

And that, if I am really truthful with you, makes me want to fuck stuff up. It makes me reckless, dangerous to myself and others.

I saw this in the girls I taught writing to in juvenile hall, and I realized I was no different from them. We were all dangerous because we had been abandoned in one way or another, only I'd had a second set of parents that had my back and saved me time after time, while these girls only had the parents who let them go, and these girls had suffered the consequences.

OBJECT

Once when I was teaching writing at the juvenile hall, one of the girls wrote about being incarcerated. She read her piece out loud, and I had to think quickly about how to handle the situation. I turned to the board and wrote her ending sentence out in big letters: I WANT TO KILL MYSELF.

The juvenile hall was for girls between the ages of thirteen to seventeen. At eighteen they went to jail. The girls were often withdrawn or chatty in tight groups of two or three. Many of them would not look me in the eye. I was a teacher. I was white. I was, compared to most of them, rich. I was just another person who thought she was better than they were for countless reasons but most importantly because I could walk out of that place and they couldn't. I was the visiting writing teacher for ten weeks a year for a program called The Art of Yoga Project. This was my third year.

I decided to turn to grammar. I talked about subject, object, and verb. I told them the verb is the action in the sentence, the thing you can do: KILL. Granted, the sentence was a little complicated as

WANT was really the verb and TO KILL was an infinitive, but I needed to make a point more than I needed to teach about sentence structure, so I continued on this somewhat faulty but necessary road. The subject, I told them, does the action, so I was the subject. The object, if there is one in the sentence, is the thing that receives the action, so in her sentence, the object was MYSELF.

I wrote I on one side of the board and MYSELF on the other. "Look at that," I said. "They are not the same person."

I looked at the girl who was fifteen years old. She was not allowed to wear make-up while she was at juvie, and so she looked like a tired child in her green t-shirt and green pants, but out in the world, dressed up and made-up, she probably looked like an adult. I thought she was wonderful. If she'd had proper parenting and an uncle who didn't repeatedly rape her as a child, she probably would have been a sports star at school and the valedictorian at graduation.

I tapped myself on the chest. "I'm adopted," I said, "and sometimes this makes me feel bad about myself." The girls stared at me. I wasn't trying to teach them something. I was telling them a story, telling them something private.

"It's hard when you know at some point you weren't wanted," I said. There were twelve girls in the room, and all of them, I'd been told in our training, had probably suffered from some form of sexual abuse. I wasn't supposed to know why the girls were serving time or anything else about them aside from what they themselves had told me in class or in their writing about their past, but in our training we were informed about the rape in order to better understand the girls' backgrounds.

These girls didn't say, "But good people adopted you, right?" They didn't tell me, "You were lucky to be taken in by a nice family," because these girls weren't the queens of whitewash. They knew pain, and they didn't believe in happily ever after. They just listened. My job was to try to connect with them so they could feel free enough to open up and perhaps find some healing by writing about what was on their minds.

"There are so many ways for us to hurt ourselves," I said, and I thought about what it must be like for them to go to sleep at night in their cells knowing they were going to wake up to the same place in the morning. These girls were incarcerated because they'd done something the police and a judge had determined was bad, and they had to walk with an air of violence because they were targets of the world's hatred. Cliques quickly formed in the hall and girls fought against girls and they had to watch their backs, had to listen for insults, for threats, had to always be ready to defend themselves or their friends or their family. Their arms and necks and even faces were heavily marked with tattoos, elaborate cursive renderings of names: their boyfriend's, their child's, a dead best friend's. I couldn't hand out pens at the beginning of class because they could easily be turned into weapons. The girls used pencils we counted at the end of class to be sure all had been returned.

"I, too, have thought of killing myself, but the problem is I like," I paused to hit myself on the belly, "I. I like I. I'm funny. I'm nice. I love my daughter." I pointed to my head. "It's the myself that's the problem. Myself gets me in trouble. Myself told me it was a good idea to steal when I was a kid instead of waiting for my allowance. Myself told me to marry someone I fought with all the time."

I was already talking too much and the girls were looking around, but I was on fire. This was potentially the most important thing I had ever taught in almost twenty years in front of the classroom. I had never conceived of this idea before—it had just come to me as a way to deal with this girl telling me she wanted to kill herself. I had found an alternative way to see the problem of living in my skin: I was the person I was meant to be and MYSELF was the me I didn't like. Just talking about it was making me more at home in my skin.

I paused to think of a writing exercise I could give them to help them see the wonderfulness of their I. I also thought about how I had signed papers making me a mandated reporter and how I had to go talk to the supervisor after class and tell her about the girl's sentence. The world is often harsh, but we are also protected in surprising ways.

One of the girls raised her hand. "Did you bring your STD to class again?"

The girls were on all sorts of drugs and were fed carbohydrate rich, starchy meals that made things like paying attention difficult. "You mean my IUD?"

She laughed. "Yeah, that thing."

I'd brought in my IUD because that was the day we were supposed to address sexual ethics as a theme, and I thought really it wasn't the girls who were the problem: it was a world that didn't acknowledge the fact that when a girl got pregnant, the fault and shame were put on her, as well as the idea she should have known better, should have said no. My birth mother was a birth mother because she hadn't had birth control. I was happy to have been given life, but the fact that it had come at the expense of another person's well-being—that my birth mother had to go into hiding for the duration of her visible pregnancy to first another state with family friends and then to a home for unwed mothers to save her family from shame—was not a thought that made me feel strong in my shoes.

"It's in my bathroom on the shelf. I got in a little bit of trouble for bringing it in."

"It was cool the doctor put it in a jar and let you take it home."

"Yeah, I liked that thing. I never got pregnant when it was in there."

"How come you took it out?"

"I'm too old to get pregnant anymore."

"You still have sex?"

I made a face and the girls laughed. These classes never went as planned.

"Let's do something fun," I said. "Put *I* on the top of the paper and list all the things that you like most about yourself." I saw most of the girls' faces go dark, saw their eyes look down, and I realized they might not be able to list a single thing at this point.

"You guys like puppies, right?" The girls looked up, started talking amongst themselves about their dogs, about how cute puppies were.

"You were a puppy once, right? You were this cute little baby and you were basically just a pair of eyes in a potato. You were so adorable—just like you are now, only smaller."

I pointed to my eyes. "Be the eyes that are looking at you as a baby, and write down all the things you like about that baby. All the things you hope for it. It's the older you looking at the younger you. The eye," I paused again to point at my eye, "looking at the I." I slapped my belly for a final time.

"You're kind of crazy, aren't you?" one of the girls said.

I nodded. "That's cool," she said, and she started to write.

I had to look down. I wanted to burst into tears. I wish someone had been able to tell me I was okay when I was a teenager in a way I could have heard. It wasn't just about being adopted. It was about feeling okay about being yourself after experiencing any kind of trauma when your brain was constantly telling you there was danger ahead and that, at any moment, the other shoe was about to drop and you were going to be in deep shit.

THE THINGS THEY CARRIED

Tim O'Brien wrote a book about his time in the Vietnam War. It's deceptive because he's telling stories about different men and telling you about the girls they liked and the things that were in their backpacks like any great storyteller would, but then suddenly there are pieces of his friend in a tree and you realize this is not like any other book you have ever written. It's the best piece of heartbreak you may ever read, and yet unless you were in the Vietnam War, really, you'll have no idea what he is talking about.

I feel the same way about adoption. You may think you understand. You may have even adopted children yourself or wished you had been adopted, but it's not the same. What happened to an adopted person's brain when he was given up by his birth mother did not happen to yours. I'm not saying to give up trying to understand adopted people or to give up trying to educate yourself. It's wonderful and important that you do. I'm saying don't assume you know what it is like. Even if you have adopted all your pets at the pound. Your eyes and your brain are going to see that the child got good parents, that everything, hopefully, worked out fine. But what you won't see is the wound, and that it because, generally, adopted people hide it. Some don't even know it is there.

GHOSTS

An adoption counselor, B. J. Lifton, writes about the ghosts that surround everyone involved with adoption. For the child, there is the ghost of the person she might have been if she'd stayed with her birth mother. There is the ghost of the child the parents might have had if they could have had their own biological child. There is the ghost of the birth mother, the birth father, and the families that were attached to them.

For the adoptive parents there is the ghost of the child they might have had, and the ghost of the birth mother and birth father whose child they are raising.

For the birth mother, there is the ghost of the baby she gave up, the ghost of the birth father, who is gone, the ghost of the mother she might have been, and the ghost of the adoptive parents who are raising her child.

In my family, we tried to pretend we were normal, that there were the three children, two fair, one dark, and our mother and our father and that, because we loved each other and we were gathered together as a family, everything would be all right.

But the ghosts kept knocking.

DRUG BABY

My mother couldn't hold on to my brother John when he first arrived. He was thin and pale and squirmy. He was also beautiful: blonde and blue eyes. The baby everyone on the white planet wanted. The fact that his birth mother had done drugs didn't surface until much, much later.

PRETTY PERFECT PRINCESS ANNE

I presented no significant problems as a child. I grew up to resemble both my mother and my father. In my forties, I would learn that my younger brother called me Pretty Perfect Princess Anne. He saw the act, not the person underneath the act. No one knew that almost every day at some point I thought about killing myself because I was so tired of not getting things right.

CAN'T CROSS THE STREET ALONE

Back in first grade, I'd had a problem getting to school. I was supposed to walk the four blocks to the crossing guard, and she would lead me across High Street to the walkway between the library and the Coburn School where the troubled high school kids went. I'd cross the lot and then head down the sidewalked field to Deerfield Elementary School. But time and time again I'd break down in tears to Mrs. Mulcahey, the guard, because crossing the street was too hard for me. I'd get sick to my stomach, and she would end up bringing me back to my mom, telling her that, once again, I hadn't made it.

My parents tried to bribe me. My mother bought me a Barbie and put it in the closet. "She's yours when you cross the street," she said.

A week later I cried because I hadn't gotten the Barbie yet. My mother broke down and gave her to me even though I hadn't done it, even though I hadn't successfully walked away from home on my own.

There was a mysterious cord binding me to my mother, and it pulled at unpredictable lengths. I wanted more than anything to get away. There was a lot of tension in my house between my brothers and my parents; no one seemed to get along very well for very long, and so, for example, at dinner, I sat in the corner of the kitchen in the old blue chair while everyone else sat at the small round table that only had four red chairs belonging to it. To fit five, we had to drag in a wooden laddered-back chair from the dining room. It was unbearable for me to watch them all battle for attention, to watch my brother eat with his mouth open, to see how little control my parents had over this wild family. I was as far from them as I could be while still staying in the room. And it has been like that for me, with almost everyone, my whole life. I want to be close, part of the group, but the feeling is nearly unbearable: it's like I am skinless and sick with sensitivity, so I have to set myself at a distance to survive.

THE LADY WILL HAVE THE FISH

There was a fierce disappointment I sometimes felt about being adopted. As much as I loved my mother and father, I lived with the fact that I felt they weren't enough, that there was something more out there for me, and this greediness made me feel ashamed, and so I tried to hide it, tried to stay small with my needs. I cleaned up after myself. I always made the bed. I covered my tracks the best that I could, trying to exist as lightly as possible. I didn't go to my college graduation. I've never gone to a high school reunion. When a friend asks where I want to eat, I want to go where my friend wants to go. I hate saying what I want. I hate existing when I have to assert myself. It's so painful. When I used to teach, I would walk out of the classroom and scold myself for being so out there, so loud, so opinionated. Who did I think I was, talking to those kids like I knew what I was doing? Like my opinion mattered? I was in the boxing ring with myself all the time, trying to knock myself out, and it was exhausting.

I was like a cartwheel inside an acorn.

SHAKEN OR STIRRED

I am reluctant to write about my brother John because I have failed him as a sister. The last time I saw him was two Christmases ago at the house that was now just my dad's since my mom had died. John gave me a black porcelain vase he had bought at a yard sale and I gave him nothing because it hadn't occurred to me he would be there. He was a good sport about it—he raised his bottle of beer to me and toasted the space between us and told me he wasn't expecting anything; he was just happy to have something to give. He was overweight and sloppy in his old t-shirt and corduroy pants. I wished he took better care of himself: he was missing some teeth and was wearing a stained leather cowboy hat, and even though he talked in a loud, cheerful voice, and even though he was kind and said loving things, he wore the disaster of his life on his exterior and it was almost impossible for me to look him in the eyes. They were blue, but a blue so dark that they almost looked black; they weren't like anyone else's eyes I'd ever seen. They were the eyes of a silent creature, something not of this world, and I never knew what they were trying to say to me, but I feared it was *please*, and so I averted my gaze, focused on his mouth or his chin whenever possible.

The story my mother used to tell was that the day after John arrived, I asked when he would be going back. I asked that question for the rest of our childhood. John wanted my love and I wanted to be left alone. He would follow me around the house, talking, talking, talking, not bothering to take a breath or to listen to me telling him to shut up. He couldn't seem to help himself. He was like a shipwreck victim and other people were the life raft. He just had to grab hold.

John didn't care about rules or social norms, and so going somewhere with him was always risky. My father used to commute to work in Boston when we were very young, and if my mother didn't keep an eye on John he would wonder off and beg for change from strangers. He was a constant threat to the stability of our family. When I was away at college he didn't leave his room for a year and then he set his bedroom on fire.

It was hard for me to feel sorry for him because he repeatedly made things difficult. During my high school graduation party, he poured out all the soda. The unpredictability of his behavior and his apparent lack of guilt made him infuriating to me. One time I bit his ear because I wanted to kill him and I couldn't think of anything else to do. His ear was unwashed and tasted of wax and that infuriated me even more. I couldn't even bite him and get any enjoyment out of it.

When I went to Kenyon, he would send me envelopes thick with cartoons he had carefully cut from the newspaper. I didn't like cartoons much and so I didn't read the ones he sent, but I would trace the precise cuts he had made on the strips of paper and wish I were a better person. I was his sister, and he just wanted me to love him. I was so homesick at Kenyon that I wrote back to him, letters that talked about living in Ohio and going to class, and I thought that when I finally got to go home again, I would be a better sister, I would stop and listen to him, but it didn't happen. As soon as I saw him, I realized my mistake. I realized it was all a mistake—my idea that home was any better than away had been. Distance had glossed over the reality of my family and my place there. The best part of leaving home is the romantic sheen it puts on how things were, and the worst part is the return, and the remembering of why you had left in the first place.

If I showed John even the slightest kindness, he would become a tornado in my personal space. There was no middle of the road hello how are you, I wish you the best, have a nice day with my brother. There was an empty glass or a waterfall with John, so I chose the empty glass. I offered him nothing, and this pained my parents for they saw that John just wanted my love and that I refused to give it. "He adores you," my mother would say. "Can't you just try?" and I would shake my head, no. I could not try. It wasn't fair—we weren't even really related. It was so crazy that this person was my brother and, while I had sisterly protective feelings for him, I also knew that on one level we were strangers and that I could turn my back on him and lose nothing.

It hurts to be afraid of someone who loves you, someone you love despite your fear because he is your brother, someone you allow no one else to say negative things about because he is your brother, but when your brother calls your other brother whose birth father was black a *nigger* and gets away with it, you wish your parents had known more about his mother and father before they had said yes to the blond boy with the blue eyes and the wild genetics of his addict birth parents. You wish they had had a little more information so they could have been better equipped to handle this baby boy who was in so much pain.

LETTING GO

Why couldn't I have stayed in our first rented house with Keats? Why did I move us so many times? Why did I have to keep bringing new things in to get rid of them? I think she should write a book called *How to Not Let Your Mom Who Was Adopted Give Away Your Shit*. I would find it unbearable to read—I mean what mom gives back her daughter's *puppy*?—but it might be good to get it out of her system, to have a group of readers who could empathize with her, tell her it wasn't her fault. That her mom was sort of busted inside and was doing the best that she could. That when she, Keats, has a place of her own, she can get all the animals and things she wants and no one can take them from her.

Letting go of a pet, like letting of a boyfriend or even letting go of a friend, (or should I say *getting rid of? dumping? abandoning?*) is a way, I think now, to feel temporarily in control. It's both a way of recreating the gut-fall of losing something you love (even if you choose to be the one to break up with a boyfriend or give away a dog, you are still losing the warmth of his presence), and a way to jolt yourself out of the numbness of almost-living to a place of sharp pain. At least you know you are alive because you hurt so much.

AND THEN SHE LEFT

I always thought I would have no problem when my daughter left for college. I wanted her to be able to leave me; I wanted her to grow up independent and strong, and then her father and step-mother and I dropped her off at college and I went back home and the silence was complete. It was as if someone had put a glass cloche over my life.

I don't remember the doctor cutting the umbilical cord when my daughter was born—it didn't seem to alter our connection at the time. She was right there, red and wet and needing me, but when I came home from Berkeley without her that day, I felt that the cord had been cut, and if it hadn't been me who'd done it. My feelings surprised and overwhelmed me. I felt abandoned and angry that she could leave me that easily. Hadn't all those years meant anything? Didn't she need me?

I decided I must have been a terrible mother because it was

like she had never been there at all. I didn't *feel* her any more.

I thought maybe that was another form of attachment disorder: the inability to feel the love that never left.

STAY WITH ME

The way I see it is that when the separation between mother and child happens a reactive tightness occurs somewhere in the child's (and likely also the mother's) body, and when the body tightens, blood flow is inhibited and there is subsequent lack of vitality. If you answered the door to find a policeman there to tell you your child died, your brain will receive the information, and so will your body. When you are a baby or a child, and your mother suddenly disappears, the panic will manifest itself somewhere in your body: the intestines may clench; the psoas may tighten; the pectorals may rotate inward to protect the heart. These patterns can remain until death. The body remembers trauma, and there are methods, such as trauma release exercises, which allow the body to do what animals do, shake off the muscle memory and bring relaxation and freedom.

In a video on somatics and trauma release, Peter Levine works with a soldier who has muscular ticks in his neck and shoulder that jerk his face to the side. Levine demonstrates how, when the soldier was in Iraq and the bomb had gone off, he would have turned his face to the side and lifted his shoulder to protect himself, and, because he'd never had a way to release the trauma, the nervous system was now stuck in that pattern. The trick was to catch the sensation in the body just before the muscle spasm occurred and to retrain the nervous system that it was safe to relax.

I wondered if this translated to infants given up by their birth mothers. I wondered what position the body would have been in when the infant realized the mother was not there. Chances are good the baby was in a fetal position, and the intestines would then be in a contracted state. Perhaps then the fear of abandonment kept the abdominal contents in this contracted state which could help explain why stomach issues were a problem for many adoptees.

GIRLS

It wasn't until I started teaching writing at the girls' juvenile hall as an adult that I saw people who carried the same basic impulse I did. During our training session the other teachers would marvel at the girls' repeated bad choices: drunk driving, repeated drug use, unprotected sex with multiple partners; the girls compulsively ruined any opportunity given to them.

All of these girls in one way or another had been abandoned by their mother, and the result, at least for me, and I think for them, was the driving need to throw themselves away again and again in the effort of finally getting it right. For if your mother threw you away: if she left you, if she hurt you, even unintentionally, some part of your brain is going to think that was the right thing to do, and you'll go down that abandonment path again and again while people talk to you about personal responsibility and self-love and pride, and even though their words sound nice and give you some hope, that one damaged piece of your brain informs the marrow of your bones, the root of all your actions, and so you don't have a chance in hell of not fucking that guy who is going to hurt you and then drive away because the mother voice in your brain told you that was a good idea, told you that you are disposable, and at the end of the day, you are a good girl and you listen to your mama.

186

I LOVE MY MOM

The stress of being our mother was clearly a terrible burden for her, and I didn't know how to fix it. There was always too much for her to do, too many things on her list, and not enough time. She would go and go and go until she got pale and sick and went to bed. This happened all during my childhood until she got cancer for the first time when I was in college and it looked like she might die. I hated her then, hated her weak handhold, hated that she was vulnerable and wan and sometimes needed help getting in and out of the car. I hated that she had her chemo and then had one of us drive her to work. She was still going to do it all, even though she threw up on the way down the street. I tried to be loving because she was my mother and she was in pain, but mostly I was furious. I believed she had brought this on herself—for how much stress can a body take before it turns on itself?—and now she was going to leave us.

My fury confused my sick mother, and she would look at me with sad eyes, but she never scolded me or told me to knock it off. She just let me be a jerk. If I could go back in time, I would stand before her and bawl, whispering *I'm so scared, please don't die, please don't die,* but I had the chance to do that some twenty years later, when she had cancer again, and that time I got it right, that time I lay next to her in her bed and bawled my eyes out and told her how much I loved her and I stroked her back and she told me she loved me, too. And she cried with me because we both knew that this time the cancer was going to win; this time she was going to die.

But if you are a Type A woman who is used to fighting her way through things, death isn't going to come easy and it isn't always going to be polite. One time when I was in the room my father bent over to adjust her pillow and my mother took his face with both hands and looked him in the eye as if about to proclaim her love. She lightly shook his head from side to side and said, "You are my stupid boy."

My father was thin and his hair was uncombed because he spent almost all of his waking hours as a caretaker. He took my mother's hands in his hand and held them and looked at her with a fatigued resolve I'd never seen in him before. "Please don't call me that," he said, and he placed her hands on her belly and went downstairs to get her more juice.

When my mother was too sick to get up on her own, she asked

me to teach her leg strengthening exercises because she didn't want my father to have to help her to the bathroom every time she had to go. She was on morphine at this point and was loopy. She would frequently call out my father's name as she had all my life "Frank!", drawing out the F, hitting the high note on the N. My father never complained. He was there with ice, with her drugs, with the desire to make sure she was as comfortable as possible as this cruel disease swelled her abdomen and ate her from the inside. I told my mother it was not time for leg strengthening exercises, and that she was focusing on the wrong thing. It wasn't about getting better any more. It was about dying. She turned her face from me and closed her eyes.

My mother was never good about not getting her way and death's door had done nothing to change this. She still had her silent tantrums, but I was okay with this now; my heart was all business. I brushed the hair from her warm forehead and watched her breathe. In her refusal to die, she was killing my father. She was wearing him ragged as she clung and clung and clung to a life that was almost out the door.

I had flown back and forth from California to New Hampshire almost every six weeks for the two years that my mother was seriously ill. Every time I left the house in Exeter to head to Logan Airport, I would hold on to my mother and cry. One time she got frustrated with me and said, "I'm still alive. Everyone acts like I'm dying, but I'm still here. I wish we could focus on that."

But now she was dying, and I was flying back every two weeks. I wanted her to die. The last time I saw her, she said, "Things have gotten worse, and I blame you. Ever since you told me you wouldn't teach me exercises I have gotten weaker." I was surprised because my mother was usually not so direct in her thoughts. But if she wanted to be direct, then fine. "You're missing your death," I told her. "You are so busy fighting it that you are missing what is happening." My mother looked at me with her eyes that were never of the world, never fully in it, and I saw that she loved me and that I was a disappointment. There was so much distance between us that it was like neither one was truly in the room.

I put my hand on the flat of her chest the way she used to do to me when I was a child falling asleep and I felt the small bones rise and fall with her breath. Soon there would be no more air in this body. Soon she would not be there anymore. I loved my mother so much. I cried and she closed her eyes and slept as the tears rolled down her face.

PLEASE COME BACK

My mother died the day before my birthday. My father called me as I was getting ready to go to a Christmas party with my husband, and as soon as I picked up the phone I knew what my father was going to say. I got a red eye that night and my father and brother and I went to see her body the next afternoon.

My father had seen the caretakers come to the house and put my mother into a body bag, so he didn't need to see her again. Sam and I left him in the waiting room and went to the room where our mom was. It was like a Las Vegas hotel for dead people, white marble and ashtrays everywhere. The coroner had told my father that we could bring special items to be cremated along with my mother, and my brother and I had picked the Mary Oliver book of poems my mother had by her bed, the king sized Snickers bar she'd had in the freezer but hadn't eaten because even dying she was conscious of her weight, and the dirty hand-worn prayer beads she'd told me to give back to the church.

My mother had her own room, and she was laid out on a table in the black body bag. This was New Hampshire, not Las Vegas, so there was a blue home-made quilt over the body bag as if she was just taking a nap inside the bag and needed warmth. My brother unzipped the bag and we saw her face and it was awful. She looked like she had been fighting a terrible beast before she died. I wanted to zip the bag closed, but my brother leaned over and kissed my mother's forehead. Our mother's.

"Is her skin cold?" I asked.

My brother touched the side of her stiff face. "Yes," he said. "But it's still her."

I leaned over to kiss her forehead. "She feels like raw chicken." He laughed and covered his mouth. I had loved my brother from the first moment I saw him. He had on a brown striped shirt and his hair was curly and hard not to touch. He walked into our house with the social worker and he was like a shy baby puppy, and I claimed him: I was his sister, his mother, his protector. I was a pain in the neck for him most of his life. I thought I was the boss. I thought he was mine to protect, but he already had a mother—he'd *had* a mother and now he had a *new* mother and he didn't need a bossy older sister who thought she'd make the best mother of all telling him what to do. But I never stopped, and so after a lifetime of me being up in his business and him keeping me at arm's distance, here we were, telling our mother goodbye and somehow he had stepped into the role of adult and I was the child. His love for our mother was greater than mine in that moment, and he unzipped the bag more, took her hand, gently opened her fingers and put the prayer beads on her palm. "Here, Mama," he said. "We love you."

He looked at me. "Can I have a moment?"

I went out of the room and stood by the door in the air-conditioned hallway. I heard my brother's gasping cries but my eyes were dry and I listened and realized I had no idea who my brother was. I thought our mother was *my* mother. But she was also his.

BEHIND THE CURTAIN

This is an example of what you get when a friend of a friend introduces you to someone she knows who is adopted and you write to that person and ask her to tell you about her life after telling her about your own.

My life isn't normal or conventional and I struggle to participate in it a good deal of the time. I'm nearing middle age and I don't have a "thing" that I do. I identify with the things I am to other people because that is how it all started. I was no thing to my birth mother and I am some thing to my parents, my sister, my aunts and uncles and cousins, to my best friend, my husband, my kids. But I am not a thing to myself. I'm quite cozy under that blanket. I don't have to feel or be deep and I can say FUCK whenever I want to. BUT...my kids are grown and my son is a disaster. My daughter is always ill. My husband is a wonderful man but I know he loves otherness more than togetherness. Sometimes it all gets me so down (insert Captain and Tennille medley here). But I was NO thing to my birth mother. Nothing erases that.

I am half good at a lot of things. As a child of "society" I took piano, tennis, horseback riding and saxophone lessons. I learned to swim, sail and ski practically before I could walk. I know which fork to use and how to make pleasant conversation at black tie affairs. I know how to dress and what jewelry to strap to myself, should the need for sparkle arise. I have mastered the expectations of my environment. I hope someday I fit in.

HERE I AM

My mother used to tell a story about how, as a child, she would organize her younger siblings and present a play to the adults at Christmastime where my mother would have the starring role and, as far as I could gather, most of the speaking parts. My mother came from the generation who told women two things: speak up and be quiet. Be big and be small. Be big like Gloria Steinem but starve yourself so you can also be beyond reproach physically. Have a big presence like Jackie O, but whisper. Read *Fear of Flying*, but only have intercourse with your husband. Not so much different from my generation, but the novelty of the value of a woman's voice was newer then. Getting attention was something my mother both craved and feared. She wanted to be in the spotlight, but she'd also grown up at a dinner table where the rule was *be seen and not heard* and with a father who thought secretarial school was a much smarter choice than Smith College. Luckily for my mother, she got a scholarship so it finally didn't matter what her father thought.

So attention and accomplishments were double sided for my

mother. She craved them, was hardwired for success with her quick brain and high energy, but she was also ashamed of showing off, of stepping out of the 1950's box women had lived in with pent-up frustration. When we'd all be in the car and one of us would start singing, my mother's voice would always be loudest. She couldn't help herself. We'd get quieter, she'd get louder until finally she was happily singing all alone.

My mother liked to do the *New York Times* crossword puzzle in pen. She had great confidence in her schooling and reach of facts. She had no self-confidence, and the combination meant that she spoke a lot, but she kept her eyes closed as if she was reading the words on the inside of her skull. It meant she felt things could be different: she believed she shouldn't have to work full time and be a full-time housewife even though that was what she when I was a teenager, even though she was proud of her accomplishments, proud that she accomplished far more in a day than my father did. Proud and angry and resentful.

It didn't surprise me, then, the subject of her fascination and posthumously published book was Louisa Adams, the wife of John Quincy, for Louisa, while she adventured and accomplished much that had gone historically unsung, also suffered from repeated physical maladies which drove her to bed, and she had titled the memoir of her adventures in Prussia *The Adventures of a Nobody*.

My mother said she'd been riveted by Louisa's gaze in her portrait that hung in the Quincy National Park. She wanted to know why no one had written a book about a French woman who had married an American President and travelled across Prussia in the winter with only servants for company.

I wish my mother had written about herself. She spent the final years of her life chasing after the details of a woman who was famous because she married someone famous. I wish my mother had written herself famous, had put the details of herself on the page so that I could see what it means to be a mother, but not a mother from a century ago. A mother now.

FUNERAL

At my mother's funeral, which she, of course, had choreographed, I read Mary Oliver's poem *When Death Comes*. I was fine until I hit the last part, and then I couldn't speak. My high school friend Susan caught my panicked eye and she touched her fingers to her lips and she closed her eyes and nodded. I took a deep breath and read even though I was crying and was speaking in a choppy whisper. *When it's over, I want to say: all my life I was a bride married to amazement. I was the bridegroom, taking the world into my arms. When it's over, I don't want to wonder if I have made of my life something particular, and real. I don't want to find myself sighing and frightened, or full of argument. I don't want to end up simply having visited the world.*

What made me cry was that I thought my mother was trying to tell everyone she'd lived the life she had wanted to, but I had seen her face when my brother unzipped the plastic body bag in the funeral home, and she did not look like a bridegroom taking the world into his arms: she looked like she had seen the light and she was furious at what it was bringing her.

I had spent almost my entire life trying to get both as close to and as far away from her as possible. In my twenties I drove across country nine times, bouncing from coast to coast: close, far, close, far. Nothing was right, I was either too close or too far, and so I kept moving.

198

And then she died and my brain stopped working normally. I fought endlessly with my second husband and we ended up in divorce court. I moved from a house to a room in a house. I worried about my finances. I cried every time someone tried to teach me something new. I would look at the hands on a clock and have no idea what they meant. I lost track of what day it was, what month, what year.

I'd be driving to work and I'd forget how to get home or I'd see a close friend and have no memory of her name. I got fired for crying in front of my class and throwing a pen at a student. My relationship with my daughter turned uncomfortable. I couldn't feel like myself in front of her and kept apologizing. She came over less, spent more time at her father's.

What I was grappling with, what was slowly suffocating my brain, was that my worst fear had come true: my mother had disappeared. I thought that maybe I would die. Every pain was cancer, every confused thought a brain tumor. I kept going to the doctor, and he kept telling me I was fine. But I knew he was wrong. I knew I was in trouble.

ARE YOU CRAZY?

I was packing up some of the things from my mother's office after she had died, but the porcelain doll wasn't on the bookcase. I went to ask my dad if he knew where it was, and he paused and said he must have thrown it away.

She was an elegant doll. Her eyes closed and she had tiny white teeth. Her legs and arms rotated in their sockets and she wore a silk slip under her soft brown dress. She had high heel shoes painted on her feet. She had a straw hat and hair in thick braids. I'd stepped on one of her legs when I was young and, after years of having a band aid keep the broken bits together, my mother had taken her to a doll repair shop in Boston where they fixed the leg and dated her from the 1890's. They said that if her leg hadn't been broken, she would have been rated in excellent condition and would have been worth several hundred dollars, but as she was—repaired—she was probably worth between one and two hundred. I would have thought she was worth at least a thousand. She was so perfect.

The miracle about the doll was that I had found her in the back of my bedroom closet when we moved into the old white colonial. I was seven and had a bedroom of my own for the first time since having a brother. The closet was narrow and had some high shelves on one end. I stood on tip toe and saw the doll sitting there, looking at me.

The previous owner had been a doll collector, and when my mother contacted her, she said I could keep the doll. I could not believe my luck. When I tilted her back, her eyelids closed. I liked to lift up her dress and touch the soft brown silk of her slip. She was the most beautiful and strange thing I owned.

When I went to college, I left her behind because the risk of travel seemed too dangerous for her fragile porcelain self, but my parents brought her with them when they moved, and she because a permanent fixture in my mother's office, reminding us of where we used to live, of our past.

After my mother died, my father had the three children come to the house one weekend so we could go around and tag the things we wanted after he had died. We didn't fight about anything; it was awkward to put a yellow stickie with our initials on it while our father was standing right there, watching. *This will be mine when you die*, the stickie said, and none of us really wanted to put a stickie on anything, but we did because our father had asked us to and because, truly, there were things each of us wanted. But when it came to the doll, sitting with her legs out in a V on the top of the bookcase, there was no discussion. My brother just walked by and put an A sticker on her lap.

"I'm sorry," my father said as I stared at him in disbelief. His wife had been dead for a year and he still sometimes cried when he talked about her, but he was already dating her best friend and was finding great happiness in the ashes of his previous life. "I was just trying to clear stuff out."

I imagined his hand grabbing hold of the doll, holding her delicate torso, carrying her over to a trash bag, throwing her in, knocking her hat askew. The image kept playing in my mind. I slapped myself on the leg and started sobbing. I couldn't stop hitting myself or yelling at my father. "You threw her away? How could you have done that? I have had her since I was seven years old! She survived since 1890 and then you just throw her in the trash?"

My father stood and listened to me and I saw his face as it must have looked when he was a child and his mother was yelling at him for bad behavior. He looked stoic, a little afraid, and a little bored. Like, *I've heard this all before, can I go now?*

I felt like I was going to throw up my heart. I couldn't get angry enough to get all the feelings out, so I ran down the stairs to the cellar where I could scream unobserved. I didn't know what I was going to do. I was afraid I might start punching the walls, tearing up the carpet. There was so much pain in my stomach. I got onto my knees on the cellar floor and rolled into a ball and sobbed.

The more I cried, the more upset I got. It was like I'd been holding a Niagara Falls of grief inside and had just found the spigot. It came to a crescendo when I thought about the fact that my father was not alone in getting rid of stuff: every pet my daughter ever had I had given away. Her puppy. Her cats. Her rabbit. Her fish. I would buy them for her in the hopes that somehow they would make her life better. That they'd provide her something to love, some comfort, some fun, but then they would chew on the furniture or pee on the rug and I'd realize that she didn't seem to care that much about them anyway. I was the one to feed them, to clean the cages, and I'd say, I think we should get rid of the bird or the turtle because they are too much work and you don't seem to care for them, and she'd shrug and out the animals would go.

It made me sick to think about what I had done. I was the worst mother on the planet, and so I cried for all of it, for the damage I had done to my daughter and for the loss of my doll. I went to bed that night with eyes as swollen as a fighter's.

My father and I tiptoed around each other for the next few days until I flew back home to California. I couldn't stop seeing the image of his hand putting the doll in the garbage bag.

A month later my father called me to say he'd found the doll. He'd packed her in a box and had forgotten. I told him he could do whatever he wanted with it. I didn't want her.

VAGUS NERVE

Our first feelings of safety are processed in the lower parts of our brain through the Vagus nerve. In Latin, Vagus means wandering. It's like a series of roadways that travel all through the upper body. This is a crucial nerve in regards to a person's sense of well-being, and the more I read about it, the more I couldn't believe there isn't a class in high school on it as generic as P.E.

The Vagus nerve goes from the lower part of the brain and it affects the tongue, the pharynx, the vocal cords, the lungs, stomach, and glands (that produce anti-stress hormones and enzymes that influence digestion, metabolism, and the relaxation response) as it reaches down to the intestines.

When I was in massage school, I learned about the sympathetic and the parasympathetic nervous system. The first is like the gas pedal the second like the brakes. Many people like receiving massage because it helps them to relax, helps them activate the parasympathetic nervous system. Their breathing and heart rate slow, their mind steadies, their muscles relax. It's the opposite of Starbucks, where, for most people, the caffeine kicks up the heart, the anxiety, the flight or fight response—the sympathetic nervous system.

The Vagus nerve is part of the parasympathetic nervous system, and it can be stimulated by a wild variety of things such as deep breathing, singing, laughing, immersing your face in cold water, doing loving kindness meditation, having positive social relationships, gargling, doing yoga or tai chi. Yes! I said gargling. This is a crazy nerve. The more I read about it, the more I loved it. Calming the nervous system was a mouthful of water away.

If as a newborn an adopted person experiences stress and a

lack of safety through the Vagus nerve and then continues to view the world through this distorted lens, wouldn't it make sense that as a child or an adult the issues of trauma and stress could be addressed and possibly reversed through this same nerve? I don't know the answer, but I'm trying it in my own life, and the results have been astounding.

For one thing, when I went to New York and started writing about adoption, my voice changed. It got deeper, and everyone who knew me thought I had a cold, but I think my throat had relaxed and my voice that was once tight and slightly squeezed was now coming from somewhere lower in my chest. I felt more like myself when I spoke. It made me feel calm, solid, real.

The Vagus nerve, it turns out, affects the vocal cords.

WRITE OR DIE

I did a writing exercise where I pretended I only had five minutes left to live, and that I had God's ear close to my lips. I was surprised by what I wrote. The first thing I said was "I'm sorry." I was sorry that I had been given the opportunity to fully flower as myself and that I had remained budded. I wrote that I wished I had not worried about money and that I wished I had spent more time on relationships. I wished I had been more present for my daughter, for everyone important in my life. For the postman, for the barista. For every being with whom I came into contact.

This exercise changed everything for me. I decided I would try to live as if I only had five minutes left. I would go into debt, but I would fully flower. I would become entirely myself and I would love people with all my heart. I would enjoy the time that I had and write until I had created the book I had so desperately needed to understand myself. The book that might have helped me see that I wasn't crazy and I wasn't alone: I was adopted.

I woke up the morning after doing the writing exercise with the image of being born. I'd never let myself go there before, and so I breathed slowly, trying not to panic the imagination away. I pictured baby me surviving the terrible squeeze of birth and feeling the doctor pass me to a waiting set of hands. I pictured myself opening my eyes to see a person that looked nothing like anything my fetus brain had created. A person who didn't sound or feel like anything I'd heard or felt before, and this white dread of aloneness swept over me.

So now I knew what the root of abandonment felt like. This was nothing I'd ever read about before, nothing I'd seen in a children's book, nothing a therapist had ever talked to me about. I grabbed a notebook and quickly sketched the story that was in my head. I named the main character Baby Momo because once Keats had done a drawing of the two of us as stick figures under a rainbow when she was a little girl, and above it she had written, *I love momo*.

THE BABY MOMO STORY

Baby Momo liked the sound of her mother's heartbeat. Baby Momo liked the sound of her mother's voice: *I can't wait to have this thing and get my life back to normal.* Baby Momo even liked the sound of her mother's tears falling: *I am never drinking that much again. I don't even know his name.* Baby Momo loved her life.

But then things started getting uncomfortable.

And then, there was light. Baby Momo heard her mother's voice very loudly: *That really hurt!*

But then the voice and the heartbeat disappeared. When Baby Momo woke up, someone was holding her and crying happy tears.

"I'm your mother," the voice said. "And this is your father. And you are our Baby Stephanie."

"STEPHANIE!?" thought Baby Momo. "What happened to Baby Momo? And WHO THE FUCK ARE YOU?"

Years later, Stephanie pretty much forgot about Baby Momo. She had her mom, her dad, and her dog Gerbil.

But she didn't really forget. She just didn't know what to say. No one had taught her the words to talk about the herself that was no longer there.

When Stephanie would tell her friends she was adopted, they would say, "So your parents aren't your real parents?" Her parents were real. Stephanie could touch them. They felt real. She loved them. Her mother tucked her into bed every night. Her father taught her how to ride a bike. She didn't remember a life before her parents. If her parents weren't real, what did that make Stephanie? "They're my real parents she would tell her friends. They're just not my birth parents."

"So they're your parents, but not really really your real parents they would say, almost in a whisper. Sometimes Stephanie would look in a mirror and wonder, "Who the fuck am I, and what happened to Baby Momo?"

BAD GIRL

When I was a kid, I'd go to the corner market and steal packs of Hubba Bubba. Writing this story, especially the work *fuck* gave me that same breathless thrill. I felt I'd either written something really meaningful or something really stupid—maybe I was a good person for writing this story; maybe I was a bad person, but all I knew for sure was that I felt really alive.

And then things got amazing.

PUT IT ON THE CARD

The next day I was walking downtown and looking at my Facebook page. Laura Munson, an author whose memoir I had read a few years earlier was suggested as a friend, so I sent a request along with a note telling her how much I'd loved her account of her crumbling marriage and how I was unable to write my own book about being adopted.

Within minutes she'd messaged me back that she had a

writer's retreat in Montana a month later and that I should consider attending as a spot had opened because of a cancellation. I had an unused emergency credit card in my wallet, and an hour later, after talking with Laura on the phone while standing outside of Whole Foods, I maxed out the card and reserved my spot and got a plane ticket to Kalispell. It was nearly three months' worth of rent.

Things always seem to happen very quickly when I make a real decision, but it doesn't become apparent that a decision is real until events happen in ways that are hard to explain. It seemed to me that the decision to bloom and write had been real and that I would be a fool not to take what was offered me even if it did come at a high price. It didn't seem a coincidence that the limit on my credit card and the price of the retreat and the flight were almost the same. I was either going to believe in some kind of destiny and have an adventure, or I was going to play it safe and stay at home.

It didn't really feel like a choice any more.

PURPOSE

I had been to Montana before. Almost thirty years earlier,

Ryan and I had driven from graduate school in Oregon to Massachusetts, and we drove through Montana because I was working on a story about an actress on a soap opera. The actress's name was Montana, and for some reason I thought I needed to see the state in order to better understand her.

We had gotten engaged because he was afraid what would happen after graduation: he would go home to California and I would go home to Massachusetts and we would probably drift apart and never see each other again. When I went in to talk to my advisor about graduation, he saw the gold band on my finger and said, "What's this?" I told him about my engagement, and there was just a moment where he looked at me, and it was a sad scolding, and we both knew one reason I was getting married was because it was easier than trying to make it on my own as a writer.

The irony is that it took two divorces to finally corner me enough to find the courage to do what I was too fearful to do in my twenties and thirties and forties: live like a writer and tell my story. I did everything I could do to avoid writing this book, but the universe or some force was not going to let me get away, and so here I am, getting it all down. It's hard now to remember what I was so scared about—I think mostly it was that the idea of having a real voice that seemed impossible. How could I be a writer when I had no idea who I was? Having a daughter helped. Finding my birth mother helped. Writing a movie and having it up on the big screen helped. Having an author who made millions of dollars on her own book lend me her apartment so I could write helped. All of those things gave me confidence and a sense of self I hadn't had when I was in graduate school. They were the antidote to *abandonnmentitis*.

MONTANA

I was picked up in a black limousine outside of the post office the morning I was headed to Montana. Another member of the group had contacted me from Santa Cruz to ask if I needed a ride to the airport. He had a car service, he said, and he could come get me.

I had less than two hundred dollars in my bank account, but I was living like a millionaire.

The retreat was something out of *Travel and Leisure* magazine: a handful of women and one man, all gathered for five days in a log cabin on a Montana lake to work on the craft of writing and to eat vegan food cooked by a woman who floated more than she walked.

Part of the retreat was an afternoon with horses and a woman who was said to be a horse whisperer. Laura said she was looking for ways to get the ten people in the group out of our heads, and for that reason she was offering the opportunity for us to spend time with Karen and her horses. "Karen is more like a people whisperer," Laura said. "Just you wait. She'll climb into your soul and shine a flashlight where you need it most."

Twenty-five years ago, when Joe and were friends, back before I knew he was robbing banks, he'd talked to me about Conrad's *Heart of Darkness*, and it was then that I learned that there was nothing I wouldn't do. I really believed that for a while, and it scared me, and for a long time after I tried to overcompensate for my transgressions by being really good.

However, I kept getting in one kind of trouble or another, usually with men or money or both and I had finally exhausted myself and those around me. I imagined my soul like a black liver, and I imagined Karen looking at all that slippery darkness, wondering where to begin.

"Did you ever work with her?" I asked.

"With Karen? I stable my horse with her." Laura started to walk away, and I touched her arm.

"Yeah, but did she illuminate your soul?"

Laura turned and faced me and I saw who was boss. "The great thing about coming here is that you don't have to worry about anyone else other than yourself. Take a deep breath."

I looked at her.

"I'm serious. Take a deep breath."

I took a quick breath. I was a massage therapist. I didn't need her to tell me to take a deep breath. I knew how important they were. I wasn't going to do it just because she told me, and, also, I was afraid I might burst into tears.

"I have been trying to write a book for twenty-five years," I said. "And I'm still not sure how to do it or what I want to say." I desperately wanted a hug, for her to grab me and hold me and tell me I was special and that what was in my head was worth all the work a book entailed.

"You'll find it here. Trust me. I'm really good at what I do. You have to believe in the worth of your work."

All my adult life I compulsively changed cities, states, jobs, husbands, friends, all as a way to have as many different stories as possible, but what if the speed at which I skated over these things made my life not of worth to the reader? What if my habit of ripping out my roots as soon as I planted some was the reason I wouldn't ever have anything real to write? What if the way I had lived my life to this point not only made my life not worthy of a book but, really, not worthy of much at all?

The wise men knew their gifts had worth because gold, frankincense and myrrh were expensive. But how did you know if your story had worth?

I must have looked uneasy because it was Laura's turn to touch my arm.

"Karen has a very powerful story," Laura said, "but she doesn't want anyone to feel sorry for her. She tells you her story on the way to the farm so you can understand how she has gotten to where she is."

I imagined the story involved violence, heartbreak, loss, and desperation. I couldn't wait to hear it. "Can you tell us the story now?" I asked. "The Cliff Notes version?" I loved hearing about people who were worse off than me and who had overcome great hardship.

"It's Karen's story," Laura said. "She has to be the one to tell it to you."

"Just tell me the highlights."

"It's part of the whole experience. She'll tell you. I promise you: the experience is a life changer."

If I was going to do this thing, I was going to do it right. If Laura said we all needed horses and a white-haired woman to get us out of our heads and into the hearts of who we were so we could show up as a writer and complete the book of our dreams, then so be it. I would have eaten paste if she had said it would help because I did not want to die the way my mother had, with a manuscript three quarters of the way complete and a look of anguish on her stiff face.

BOUNDARIES

Karen was taking groups of three to her farm each day, but this day the two women in my group had decided they needed massages more than they needed to go to a horse farm, and so I was the only one climbing into Karen's old Ford after lunch that day. She didn't seem to mind that she had lost two thirds of that afternoon's income. She slapped her leg and smiled at me. "Two's company," she said.

"And three's illegal in some states," I replied.

She laughed, "We'll get along fine," she said. I wanted Karen to like me. I wanted her to tell me that I was all right, that everything was going to be all right, and that although I didn't really have a job or a man and although my child had left for college and although I often ate my take-out dinners sitting on the floor of the room I rented, that everything was happening for a reason and that I was on the right track.

On the drive up to the barn, Karen told me that when her twenty-two-year old daughter Alice was born, the doctor suggested Karen put her in a home. He told her that Alice would be too much work for Karen, and that Karen should save herself. Karen said if she had put her in a home, Alice never would have been a cheerleader in high school, never would have graduated, never would have been Karen's sidekick at the farm, caring for thirty horses and three llamas and fourteen guinea hens. Karen told me. "Alice lives 100 percent in the present moment. Most people overthink everything. Alice is right there, reminding me that this moment is the only moment. She is my greatest teacher."

Karen sat like one of those Lego figures who have a 90-degree bend at the hips and the knees. She was so close to the steering wheel she could rest her chin on it during straight stretches of road. She had darkly tanned skin and wrinkles and bones and just enough muscle to keep the whole apparatus of herself moving. I wondered what she ate for breakfast, for lunch, for dinner. I wondered if she grabbed a carrot and ran out the door, whether she skipped meals entirely to save time and money, or whether she was one of those people who could sit down to a cheesy lasagna and shovel down a couple of pieces without blinking. If I had had to guess, I would have said she lived on air. She looked like that kind of person. The kind that didn't put much stock into eating, into sitting down and feeding herself. Not when there were so many other creatures around who needed nourishment.

When we pulled up the driveway and got out of the car, Alice came strutting out of the trailer home dressed all in turquoise: tank top, sweat pants, cowboy hat. Her headphones were pink. She danced all the way across the grass to us: spinning, twerking, silently lip syncing her way from the house to the driveway. If Arnold Schwarzenegger and a dwarf had mated, they might have made this wild firecracker, but instead it had been wiry Karen and her alcoholic ex-husband.

I walked up to Alice as she raised her arms and slowly gyrated her hips. I wanted Karen to see straight off that I wasn't afraid of anything, even of a young girl with Down's syndrome who was moving like a pole-dancing maniac.

"So you're Alice," I said as she spun towards me. "I've heard all about you."

The music must have been loud because Alice didn't even blink, she kept gyrating, staring somewhere off in the distance. I stood and waited for her to finish. Her eyes were half closed and she looked like she'd dance off the edge of a cliff if that was what was nearby, if that was where the music took her.

Finally she did two long, slow gyrations, bending low at the knees, and then she took off her hat and bowed. I clapped.

"Take off your headphones," Karen said, miming the action.

Alice took off her headphones. "So that was me, Alice," she said. "And now you have seen it all. Thank you for coming to the

220

show." She stuck out her hand and firmly shook mine in her sweaty palm. I took her hand, held it next to Karen's.

"You two have the same hands." Alice had a compact version of Karen's tight, gnarled paw.

"Not really," Alice said. "Mine are attached to my arms."

Karen laughed.

"You should meet my daughter," I said. "She would love you."

"Where do you live?"

"California."

"Okay. I'll get in the car with you when it is time to go."

Karen cleared her throat. "But right now I am going to go inside and color," Alice said. "And you know why?"

I shook my head.

"Because I'm bored and so maybe I will stay here with you." Alice started to put her headphones on again, but then Karene cleared her throat and Alice looked at her. Karen held eye contact with her daughter and all the gentleness that was in that woman's soul was in her eyes, but there was something unquestionable and unmoving there, too, and Alice let the headphones drop back around her neck and she waved goodbye to us and she turned and walked back into the house.

"Have your eyes always that blue and luminous?" I asked Karen. Her skin was lined and dark from years of sun, but her eyes were wide and clear and new-looking. They didn't make sense. They were the eyes Karen might have had when she was fourteen and had fallen in love with her first boy.

"They've always been like this," Karen said, and she shrugged, like, they are so amazing and I know it and what can I do?

Some people get the shit kicked out of them by their parents or their husbands and by some miracle it turns to a kind of super power of love and steel. Karen had that, and I watched her every move the rest of the afternoon.

As we walked toward the corral, Karen told me that the horses could read my energy, and that the horses would read and react to the conscious and unconscious signals I sent to the world.

I imagined the horses flocking to me, recognizing the affinity I'd had with their species so many years ago as a teenager. I figured they'd see through my fear and straight to the courageous person I had once been.

"You have no boundaries," Karen said, handing me a long white whip. "We call this a magic wand."

I shook my head. "I don't need a whip," I said.

"It's a magic wand," she said, flicking it at me. "Take it."

I took the white whip like I wanted it, like it was my choice to take it. At sixty-eight, Karen could have taught a class in posture to twelve year olds, or to me.

"Mirror neurons are what help the horse to empathize," Karen said. "I yawn, you yawn: that's mirror neurons in action: monkey see; monkey do. The horses help heal people."

The sun was bright and I was wearing a black shirt and black pants. I had left my sunglasses in the truck because Karen said the horses needed to see our eyes, so I used one hand as a visor.

"The fence is live," Karen said as she unhooked a strand of wire. "Don't touch it unless you want to fry yourself."

I'd had a headache for the first two days of the retreat. I'd forgotten about the elevation, how I'd gone from 100 feet above sea level to 6,000. My headache had faded on this, the third day, but I was starting to feel closed in on, dizzy.

"That's George," Karen said, pointing to a small light brown horse grazing off by himself. "He was badly abused before we got him. We let him be a horse and now he seems to be doing okay. He never would have come this close a year ago. See his ears?" Karen said. "How they are pointed in this direction? He's monitoring us without even raising his head."

I sent out my love to George. *I am fearless and I love horses and you are going to come to me*, I telepathically communicated to him. *I have taught writing to girls in juvenile hall*, I continued. *And they most of them were seriously fucked up by their parents. You are safe here. Everything will be okay.* He continued to graze while the handful of other horses in the corral grazed, also. None of the them were coming to me. I felt white around the edges, like I was being erased by the hot sun and dusty air. I crouched down as if I were a baseball coach, intent on watching the game from a different angle.

"You okay?" Karen asked.

"Yup," I said. "Squatting is good for the back."

Karen looked at me and I imagined the horses thought she was twelve feet tall.

"I'm feeling a little faint."

Where had the me I used to know gone? I couldn't even

remember how to touch a horse. They seemed like big lipped, heavy-footed, unwieldy things to me now. Petting one would be like petting a hot water heater: foolish and awkward. But there had been a time when I would go to the horses in the barn and drape myself over them like I was a blanket or a second skin. I remember the smell, the warmth, their heart and my heart and the sound of contented breath.

"Actually, I might throw up," I said.

Karen came over to me and touched my back. "Let's get you to some shade," she said. "God may mess with us, but we can mess with him right back. I promise you, after today, you'll never be the same."

"I thought I was fine. I don't know why I'm so dizzy," I said.

Karen looked at me and shook her head. "You are fine," she said. "But we all have our stuff. And that's all it is: stuff. But sometimes it takes over."

"I have been trying to write about adoption since I was a teenager," I told her, wondering if I would know I was going to faint before I actually did. I wondered if I would hold my hands out or if my face would hit the ground at full velocity.

"It sounds like that's a tough one for you."

It was so nice to hear someone say that instead of, "What's so hard about that?" I thought about the first time I tried to write about who I was for a college entrance essay. I remember saying I felt like a flowing river, but that there was a stick blocking the water from easy movement. I had no idea what that stick represented or what it even meant to be stuck. I knew something was not quite right, but I didn't have the words to talk about it directly, so I talked about running track instead, what running the third lap of the mile felt like because I wanted to show that I had tenacity and a winner's spirit even if a lot of the time the third lap was when I gave into coming in second or third.

"I am scared of these fucking horses."

"These horses should not be fucking," Karen said in a steely voice. "This is a no fucking farm."

I laughed. I started sweating and I hoped she was joking because it was going to be the last straw if my laughing made her mad at me: what if my broken marriage had followed me all the way to Montana and I made not just my husband mad but everyone around me? I didn't think I could take even one more bit of anger in my life.

She patted my arm and smiled. "Come on," she said. "I know

what you need. Let's introduce you to Gracie."

She took me to a small brown horse and had me stand at her side. "Just let her get used to you," Karen said. Grace moved her heavy head to smell my stomach, my shoulders. She tapped my chest with her nose.

Karen said, "She is usually standoffish with people, but I had a feeling about her with you. She knows you're all heart." I looked at Grace, at her sweet, soft eyes, and I hoped she was right.

A rangy black horse came running towards us and Gracie stumbled away. "That's Stanley," Karen said. "He thinks Gracie's his. I want you to stand there and open up your arms. Show him you are boss."

I didn't want to stand there and open up my arms. I wanted to run, but Karen's voice didn't offer room for choice. I hated that I was dizzy and sweating, and that a skinny horse was about to trample me, and that I had paid a lot of money for this experience. I wanted to yell at Karen, but I had the whip in my hand and I figured if worse came to worse I'd just whip the shit out of him if he started bucking me or whatever crazy business he had planned. I stood there and opened my arms like I was stopping a Mack truck in traffic and Stanley skidded to a halt. Karen whooped. I felt like a superhero. Stanley whipped his tail in annoyance and ambled off.

"That's what boundaries feel like!" Karen shouted.

I felt huge.

IN YOUR FACE

One time, when my daughter was a little girl, her doctor told her it was time to stop sucking her thumb because she was throwing her jaw out of line. We talked about it on the way to the car. I told her we could have a candy day—we'd go to the store and buy a bag of candy and every time she wanted to suck her thumb, she could have a sweet instead. The next day, I said, would be toy day if she was able to not suck her thumb on candy day. On toy day we would go to her favorite store and she could pick one toy. Anything. We'd figure out what to do on day three later.

She nodded. She was such a reasonable kid. Later that day, I picked her up to hug her and she stared at my face. She looked quietly desperate. "Can I suck your nose?" she asked.

I swallowed my laugh and nodded. She looked at me like she

was about to kiss me. I wanted to swallow her whole. What do you do with that much love? The feeling was nearly unbearable, and it would have been as easy to explode out with a list of expletives as it would have been to pass out from joy. She leaned in and put her lips around my nose, and sucked. I breathed through my mouth, trying not to laugh, trying not to die from happiness, from the wet feel of tongue around the small curves of my nose.

She was mine. And yet I wanted her closer still. I wanted one of us to climb inside the other, feel the slide of blood, the home of bones.

Galway Kinnell has a poem called *The Bear* where the narrator climbs inside a bear's carcass. I understand that longing, that marrow need for in.

> *I hack*
> *a ravine in his thigh, and eat and drink,*
> *and tear him down his whole length*
> *and open him and climb in*
> *and close him up after me, against the wind,*
> *and sleep.*

I have never been as close to anyone as I have been to my daughter, and yet ever since she became a teenager, and especially since she left for college, the distance between us is unchartable. I don't even know if she likes me. She keeps her life largely to herself—she's Instagram and snap chat, laughter while she looks at her phone. In so many ways I have no idea who she is.

I think the part of my brain that is programmed to believe that those I love will disappear doesn't know what to do with distance, both physical and mental. Almost every time my daughter texts me, she says I love you, and yet I continue to live with the uncertainty of whether she even likes me.

I have a friend who is also adopted. She has been married for twenty-two years and she told me in confidence that every day she thinks that might be the day her husband will leave her, and he has no idea she has these thoughts. You can see the unease in her eyes. It doesn't matter how big her house is, how many new clothes she has, how many times a day her kids and her husband hug her—at any moment her world could collapse. When I see pictures she posts on Facebook I see how close she sits to her husband, how she amoebas him. There is love, and then there is fear love. Fear love clings, fear love cries for no reason. Fear love can't take deep breaths, can't fly free. Fear love thinks: one day you will leave me, and then I will die.

SHARING MOMO

When the day came for me to share my work at the retreat in Montana, I decided to read the Baby Momo story because everyone else so far had read from pages that clearly meant a lot to them. The people read with shaking voices and hands, and I thought I would change the tone—read something silly and light.

I was shocked by the response.

The group moved in close while I read so that they could see the drawings on each of the flash cards, and the room looked like an elementary school with a bunch of kids sitting cross legged as the teacher read. People were laughing, but they were also crying. Afterwards, Laura pointed to the man and said, repeat the lines, *She just didn't know what to say. No one had taught her the words to talk about the herself that was no longer there.* And he did, and his eyes welled up and she said to him, "You hear that, don't you?" and I watched, dumbfounded.

"You have an important story to tell," Laura said to me, and everyone in the room nodded. That night, a woman in the group, a fabulously famous writer, told me I could have her New York City apartment as a place to write in the near future if I ever wanted. I told her thank you, but I couldn't imagine how that would ever be possible.

The way to make it possible, I found, was to say yes.

GO THOREAU

I left California because I had to go Thoreau on my life, had to leave everything that had become so familiar. I was going in circles, feeling sad more often than happy, feeling like dying might be more of a blessing than living. I had to leave California *because I wished to live deliberately, to front only the essential facts of life, and see if I could not learn what it had to teach, and not, when I came to die, discover that I had not lived.* It sounded so romantic when Thoreau did it, so easy. Throw my satchel of things over my shoulder and head for seclusion so I could find my true self.

It sounds so easy, to step out of your life, but it was one of the hardest things I have ever done. I had spent my adult life accumulating things: books, clothes, furniture, things and things and things, and now these material objects that I had worked for, had spent money for, were making it impossible for me to change, to pull up anchor and go.

How do you get rid of things you love? Things that represent who you are? The Buddha statue. The framed photographs of your daughter, your parents, your friends? The art work that you have carried with you from place to place to place, hammering new holes in the wall so you can remind yourself of what you love and who you are. So you can remind yourself that everything is okay, that even though you are in a new place, you have carried your old life into it, and the continuity of *this is who I am*—this silver candleholder, this blue rock from the beach in Maine—will continue and keep you protected within the bubble of identifying objects that murmur *here I am, here I am, here I am.*

How do you get rid of all the shit that you so carefully saved in plastic boxes and then shove under your bed: a rolodex from the 1980's. A baby dress that might be yours—you can't remember. Letters from old boyfriends. Battery chargers for batteries you can't locate but know must be somewhere. A wetsuit you used three times that your daughter might want some day. It's valuable stuff, stuff you feel you can't give away, but stuff that you don't need *right now*.

I dreamed of a fire coming and burning up everything I owned so I didn't have to sort and decide. The losing of the things wouldn't have been so terrible—I could feel like a victim of fate and publically mourn what I had lost, it was the giving away that was hard. How do you give away a picture your daughter drew when she was six? The Madame Alexander doll with the matted hair you've had since you were three? The handful of white cords that may go to something you own? How do you give away all that you have dragged behind you for years without feeling that you are desecrating the past? How do you say, I thought you were important, but watch this, watch me open my hand and let everything I held on to so tightly slide away?

But I had finally decided that if this life didn't feel right to me, then I was going to get rid of it.

I got two credit cards and started sleeping on the floor at my friend's house.

I was going to take away almost everything that was pinning me to the world. I gave away my books. Most of my furniture. There was so much I had already given away or left behind: clothes, furniture, rugs, framed art, my hammock. I'd left my All-Clad pans and Japanese knives with my ex-husband. All the plants I'd carefully potted. The china from my first marriage. The Christmas tree decorations I'd been collecting since I was a teenager.

I lived with the thought that I was doing to my daughter the very thing that had caused the most trouble for me in my life: I, her mother, was abandoning her. It was hard for me to breath when I thought about this, so mostly I tried to push the thought away, mostly I tried to tell myself you can't abandon someone who has left for college, you can't abandon someone who doesn't live with you any more, someone who is already gone.

But I knew the truth. She was at college an hour away and would be home for vacations and long weekends and I would not be able to provide her a place to stay. She had her dad's, that was true, and she was happy there. That was also true. But she might get sick at school and I wouldn't be an easy drive away. She might have to fill out a form that asked for my address and she'd have to freeze, uncertain. She might forget my face. She might think there was something unlovable about her for her own mother to up and go.

STARTING GUN

I wasn't sure how to pack. I would be gone for three months, but I was going to be dragging my suitcase around New York and Martha's Vineyard, so I took whatever fit into a small suitcase with wheels. Not much. Two pairs of jeans. A few shirts. Socks. A sweater. Underwear. I wore my coat, my loafers.

I woke up when it was still dark out, got dressed, and wheeled my suitcase two blocks down the road to where my massage office was so the taxi driver could more easily find me. It felt like the whole neighborhood was asleep. The wheels of the suitcase loudly rattled, but I didn't do anything to stop them. I was headed out to write a book. I wanted to leave some sort of trail.

It can feel so good to walk away, like taking a shower or bathing in some magic silver light. It felt so good to get in the taxi, to get out at the airport, to go through security, to sit at the windows that were still dark and to look out at the strings of planes landing and taking off and to know I was free.

I'd brought with me a questionnaire a friend had posted on Facebook from a *Modern Love* column, *To Fall in Love with Anyone, Do This*. Some psychologists had done a study to see if love between two strangers could be accelerated if they asked each other personal questions. I'd thought, since I was going to New York to write about myself, it might be good if I tried to fall in love with myself along the way, so while I waited for my plane to board, I began to answer the questions. The first one was, "Given the choice of anyone in the world, whom would you want as a dinner guest?"

I thought about Einstein, Jane Campion, Jesus. I could ask Einstein what it was like to have so many big thoughts, but since I didn't actually know much about relativity, the conversation might be stilted. I loved Jane Campion's film "The Piano" and wanted to talk about the process of writing and filming it, but she was still alive and maybe I would actually meet her in the world without giving away this wish. Jesus would be remarkable. I was uncomfortable with all the images of him nailed to the cross, but, as a massage therapist, to meet someone who could supposedly heal with a touch would be incredible. There was the issue of religion, however, and if Jesus was offended that I didn't believe in the story of his conception, the dinner might be awkward.

I tried to think about whose presence across from me would most change my life. "My birth father," I wrote.

I teared up sitting there in the airport. What I was asking for was not all that complicated, and yet it would never, ever happen. It seemed like such a gyp. Why hadn't people been more helpful? Why wasn't there some sort of national APB board where people could look for their birth mother and father? How could friends of my birth mother—even the children of my birth mother—know that there were things they could do, people they could ask, to help find out who my birth father was and do nothing?

I imagined sitting at a table in a restaurant and having a man who looked like Ken Doll approach me, look in my eyes, see himself in my face, and say, "Hello, Darling." He would be like a date and a father, handsome and attentive. We would laugh at each other's jokes and I would have to keep reminding myself that we were related by blood and to not reach for his lightly-haired wrist. I would remind myself to not look in his eyes too deeply or fall in love the wrong way.

In a week, my daughter would turn nineteen. It was the first birthday of hers I would miss.

THE WRITER'S LIFE

Fly to Boston. Stay with best friend for three days. Take the train to New York City. Stay in the East Village at the Fabulously Successful Writer's brownstone for two weeks. Get back on the train to Boston and go to best friend's house for a night. Take the T to North Station and take the bus to Woods Hole and take the ferry to Martha's Vineyard. Stay in Edgartown at the writer's colony for two weeks. Get back on the ferry; get in a car; ride to Boston; get on a train and go back to New York and write and write and write.

OPEN SESAME

I'd been instructed to go to the dry cleaners on the corner of 10th and 3rd, hand over twenty dollars, and ask for the keys to the brownstone. There were two keys; a white one for the first two doors of the entranceway and a black one for the door to the apartment itself.

I dragged my suitcase behind me, but in New York it made no noise. It was rush hour in the East Village and drivers leaned on their horns. It didn't matter that my hair was stuck to my head after the flight or that my makeup had long worn off. I'd left the perfect polish of my suburban life behind. I looked like half the people who were walking past me. Two girls were sitting and smoking on the steps of the brownstone. "Sorry," I said, as I walked around them, but they didn't stop talking, didn't look at me.

My hands were cold so it took some fumbling moments to get the key in the lock. The door opened to the mailboxes and to another heavy windowed door. I could see the curving staircase, the white walls. I felt like I was in a Woody Allen movie, and then I went inside and unlocked the door to the apartment and started mumbling, *oh my god oh my god oh my god* as I took off my shoes and looked around.

HBL

It was day 35 of Write or Die. I couldn't stop saying *fuck*. I'd left New York for the two-week residency on Martha's Vineyard, and I had walked in the April snow to the one open coffee shop in Edgartown.

What are you afraid of? HBL texted after I sent him the page I'd written that morning with a message bemoaning my ability to find a way into my story.

240

I wrote back *I am afraid that, in the end, I have no story to tell. That the lack of concrete beginning undermines the whole thing and that the project sags under why bother.*

I am afraid that I am making excuses and that instead of taking control of my life and taking care of myself financially, I'm blaming my juvenile behavior on adoption. I am afraid of looking at how inconsequential my feelings were when I was growing up. I am afraid of looking at how easily I was given away. I am afraid of how numb I am because underneath is a lot of pain and anger. I am afraid of acknowledging the fact that I think I am valuable. I have to go now, I wrote to him. *That last one made me cry.*

I had met HBL on Tinder four months earlier. His profile stated that he was married and that he traveled a lot. We didn't even live in the same state. He looked handsome and confident and so I swiped right. I was looking for men who were available, but there was something about his face. He was wearing sunglasses, so it wasn't his eyes. It was the way he faced the camera, like he was ready to take on the world, but he was leaning back in a lounge chair, so it looked as if he knew the world would come to him. Later, I asked him who had taken the photo, and he said he didn't remember. I assumed that meant his wife, and that he had been looking at her.

We went from flirting on Tinder to texting and emailing multiple times every day and occasionally talking over the phone. I preferred texting for many reasons: one was that I didn't like talking on the phone in general, but the other was that HBL's voice was higher than I had initially imagined, and it bothered me. I wanted him to sound like a doctor on TV, serious, masculine, but HBL sounded like an uncertain soprano on the phone. His texts were much more authoritative and steady, and so I did my best to keep us typing.

He had two adopted boys, and so aside from bodily desires, we had many things to talk about. After a few weeks, we met one night for dinner in my town, and there were not the physical fireworks either one of us had expected. We didn't know what our relationship was about, but we kept up our daily conversations, sometimes emailing or texting over thirty times, and he was often the first person I greeted good morning or wished good night.

The most surprising thing was the fact that he had become my editor. I would send him a page or two that I had been working on, and his comments were almost immediate in arriving and always spot on. He pushed me to write about my thoughts and feelings in a way that no other human had ever done. Even a therapist. Even friends in intimate conversations or a husband, in bed. If I'd been an animal, I would have been a cat curled on his lap, so happy for the soothing heat of his attention.

HBL stood for Hunk O'Burning Love, the name he'd sarcastically suggested I use when I told him his real name didn't suit him. His presence became like a second heartbeat in my day. I wasn't always aware of him, but he was always somehow there. Every day he wrote to encourage me to keep writing. Every day he told me I was wonderful, beautiful, special.

It was hard to know what was real. He told me his wife was bipolar and that he was staying with her for their boys, but that more than anything he wanted to leave. He told me that they didn't have sex. I wondered if I was the only woman he texted daily. I wondered if I was as special to him as he claimed.

When you are adopted, anything is possible. If your own mother had decided to give you up, who knew what else could happen. The sky was the limit. The other shoe could drop at any moment and anyone, at any time, could disappear.

But the thing with HBL was that he kept showing up. Even

when I wrote things about adoption that made him as a parent of adopted boys uncomfortable, he didn't back away. Even when I wrote that I was going on dates. He would tell me that it pained him to hear about other men, but that he knew he wasn't being realistic. He kept checking in, offering support, encouragement, love.

When we had first started texting, it was about sex. I am going to do this to you. I am going to do this when you do that. We could get each other worked up in a quick volley of messages. But by this point, we were like old lovers, *How are you, Sweetheart? How did you sleep? I wish you were lying next to me. I miss you.*

I stopped trying to figure out what to call our relationship after we met and we didn't have sex. The fact that we survived that, two people who depended on physical intimacy to connect to the opposite gender, was a miracle.

When I wrote once that I was feeling discouraged about my writing, he responded *You've said to me that I've changed your life but I've never really said that to you. That's because until the other night when Paul asked about his birthmother, I didn't realize how much you've changed my life. You have made me see the vital importance of allowing my kids to talk about their adoption, good or bad. You've made me open my eyes to the possibility that Danny's withdrawal could have something to do with active or latent feelings of abandonment he may have. What if I'd never met you? I would have been blind to that and let my kids flounder. This is why your book is important. This is why your story is important. This is why you are so damn valuable. Well, there are many, many reasons for that. But this is your work, your story, and it's infinitely more important than most.*

I probably should have written most of that in caps.

I read his message more than once. More than five times. His support kept me going. Someone was paying attention. Someone was letting me talk about adoption as much as I wanted. I was finally able to be myself.

Write or Die was working. A month in and I had written eighty-six pages and I was settling into my own skin and voice. I wrote and napped and dreamed and cried and talked with the other writers staying at the residency with me. It was the happiest time of my life.

THE FIELD BY THE HOUSE

I rented a bike in Edgartown, and when I told the guy I planned to ride to Menemsha he raised an eyebrow. "It's not an easy ride. You can call for a cab or take the bus back if you want," he said. "Both carry bikes." Two hours later, I stopped to take a picture of the fish shack we used to go to when I was a kid to sell the squid we'd caught as bait for candy money, but my phone wouldn't even turn on. My butt was sore and my legs were tired and all the stores were closed for the season and there were few cars on the road. I was going to have to turn around and ride the two hours back.

I thought about looking for the house we used to rent, about finding the field, about sitting there and imagining I was with my mom, and I remembered how I used to feel as a child, as a teenager, as an adult, when I'd go away from home and fantasize about returning, about feeling the warmth of home, the complete acceptance where I could relax and float in the safety of family love, but as soon as I was within walking distance, I would realize I had been dreaming, and that I was headed for the empty middle of the life ring.

There was no reason for me to search for the field or for my mother. She wasn't going to be there. Even when she had been there, it hadn't been enough. There was a picture of the two of us in the family photo album. My mom was crouching next to child me, and together we were holding on to the string of a kite that was visible as a tiny red triangle in the sky.

It wasn't that moment I longed for. I wanted to push through that moment, through my mother, through the distracted motherness of my mother, through her skin, her bones, to the other side. I wanted the other life. The life where I was the other me.

In the 1980's Mona Simpson had written book called *Anywhere But Here*, and I carried it around with me for years, like a Bible. The relationship between the straight-laced daughter and the irresponsible mom was essentially the relationship I had with myself, and the fact that they didn't have furniture no matter how nice or run down their homes were made me feel Mona Simpson understood the displaced, understood me. It was the title I loved most of all, however. Having it typed up on the cover of a best-selling book made me feel that the hidden song of my heart: anywhere but here; anyway but here; anywhere but here was not mine alone, and that if Mona Simpson had found value in the telling, maybe I could, too.

The ride home was painful. I hadn't worn pants with any kind of padding, and the last hour I stood on the pedals whenever I could, muttering "Ow, ow, ow." Martha's Vineyard seems small, but when you are on a bike on the off season, the roads stretch long and empty and you could as easily be on an endless road in Ohio.

When I dropped off the bike, there was a man in a Patriot's sweatshirt standing outside with the man who had fitted the bike for me. When they heard I'd made it to Menemsha and back, they looked at me. "Four hours," the bike guy said. "Impressive."

"I have broke ass, though." I said.

"I can fix that," the guy in the Patriot's sweatshirt said.

"You've probably spent time in prison. Said that to all the guys."

The men laughed. The rules were changing right before their eyes. A woman who looked like their mother was talking like a guy in the bar.

"Bend over," Patriot said. "I'll fix you."

Neither one of the guys was sure where this was going to go. They were tense and laughing. At any minute I could turn into a really bad Yelp review. "You'd be in so far over your head," I said, and hit myself on the rear. We all laughed. Life was good. We were rude and unpredictable and happy to be alive.

I hadn't found my mother, but I'd made it from one end of the island to the other and I had made two men laugh. I knew that when I handed over the bike, I wouldn't be going to the other end of the island again, at least not on this trip. I wasn't a good girl. I was nearly twenty thousand dollars in debt; I had more than one man waiting for me to return to New York. I didn't have a job; I hadn't seen my daughter in over six weeks. I had a belly. I wasn't wearing makeup any more. I wasn't going to the gym, swimming laps, hiking for hours at end. I was lying around for long stretches, writing, napping, texting different men the things I was going to do when I saw them next. I was freely saying much of what came to mind and half the things made people's heads turn, half the things made people laugh. I was getting away with being myself.

The quarter mile walk back to the writing residency was strange. It felt like I had concrete blocks for feet. Each step was an accomplishment. I wasn't happy. I wasn't sad. I was trying to walk home.

I LOVE YOU I'LL NEVER LEAVE

I left Martha's Vineyard with two of the women who had been at the writer's retreat. We were a little late because one had taken a long time to get out of the house, and she was telling us about the Italian Goodbye. We were laughing because I'd tried to get out of the house without saying goodbye to anyone, but I'd been caught. Saying goodbye meant you mattered. Saying goodbye meant you wouldn't see that person again. It was so much better to disappear.

I told them that adopted people need to hear "I love you" and "I will never leave you" on an hourly basis. For the rest of the drive, they would stop midsentence, look at me, and say "I love you. I will never leave." I laughed every time like, stop it, stop it. I felt like a kid who knew she was too old for her mother to be taking her hand to cross the street but who secretly liked the warm hold.

PUT YOUR BODY IN YOUR BODY

My father called me when I was back in New York and he told me he was going to see my brother who wasn't doing so well. He was having problems with his teeth so eating was difficult. He was having problems getting enough work and had to be careful when driving his car as it was unregistered. He had a boyfriend, but they were having troubles.

I listened to my father and wondered if my brother would have had the same problems if he hadn't been adopted. I can't help it. I see the world through the eyes that I have. I feel like my parents adopted three kids who were broken in their own ways, but the game was to pretend we were all intact, all perfectly normal. This means that my parents suffered more, perhaps, then other parents, because the behavioral problems they faced with their children might be seen as reflection of the parenting we received when that was not the case. It was the unknown genetic background and stories we brought with us that caused the problems.

I gave my father advice, told him he needed to let my brother fend for himself so he could realize he was fully independent, but I felt like a fraud. I wasn't much different from my brother. I was right on the edge of financial ruin. I was homeless. I was behind on all my payments. I didn't have a job. The irony of course was that I was staying in a multi-million-dollar brownstone and had nice clothes and a good haircut and a daughter who was a freshman at Cal and looked, I imagine, to the outside world that I was living the dream.

The urge to throw myself away was so strong, this undertow of self-destruction I'd had to fight for so long was, I feared, winning, and that perhaps I had not come to New York to build myself up as I claimed, but to break myself down.

It was coming down to choice. I could focus on my past stories and let them define what I would do, or I could focus on the moment I was living and live from that.

One time, when I was at Occidental College and having a hard time—I'd started being really careful with what I ate and weighed twenty pounds less than I normally did, only the weight was slowly coming back on and I was panicking. The only thing I had at school was my identity as a very thin person, and I felt terrified of what I was becoming.

I went to the school psychologist, and started talking to her about transferring to Occidental, about leaving Smith, Kenyon. About how I had no idea who I was or what I was supposed to be doing. About how I was trying to please my parents, but about how I wasn't going to classes all that regularly, about how I was wasting their money. I started to sweat and had the terrible feeling I was standing on the edge of a cliff. I saw, that if I wanted to, I could dive off into insanity.

"Put your body in your body," the therapist said, and I did. I pulled my body from wherever it had gone to out in the room and shoved it back into the outline of my body. It was like magic. I was back. I ended up dropping out of Occidental and gaining back all of my lost weight, but I survived.

I never forgot that moment, the fact that sanity was a choice, that at any moment I could leap off, and that the trick was to keep my body in my body.

And I think this is the essence of what the struggle is for many adopted people. The urge to relive the initial trauma, the disassociation of the body from the body that happens when the birth mother disappears. The ghost baby that chases after the disappeared mother while the flesh baby goes out of the room to live another life.

HIGH

I talked to a man who was my age who was adopted but who said he had no issues with it. "I mean, my parents are Jewish but I know I'm only 20% Jewish because I had my DNA tested, but I would never tell them that," he said. I asked why he wouldn't tell them. "I can't risk getting disinherited," he said. "They have all the money. I have one other brother, but he's natural, and they threaten him all the time they will disinherit him."

"Natural?" I said. "You just called your brother natural? What does that make you?"

He looked at me and smiled, caught.

"But adoption hasn't affected you at all," I said. "I get it."

We talked about his childhood, how he was always in trouble in school even though he was really smart, and how his mother was always yelling at him. "Maybe I had ADD or dyslexia," he said. "I used to be terrible at math."

"Are you terrible at math now?"

He shook his head.

"Would you be willing to entertain the idea that adoption might be traumatic and it might affect children's behavior and ability to focus?" I asked.

He looked uncomfortable, like I was asking him to take the last pastry off a plate.

"Maybe," he said. "I used to not tell anyone I was adopted. Sometimes I would even lie about it, but as soon as people saw me with my family they knew. I mean, look at me." He gestured to his tall, heavy-set body. His red hair. "My parents are small and Jewish," he said. "Tiny."

I asked him if anything would compel him to read a book about adoption. He shook his head slowly. "I mean, if it was a book everyone was reading, then maybe, but otherwise? I mean, why?"

The more we talked, the more I saw that the all the unspoken feelings and issues and thoughts about adoption can build up in a person like water in a closed hose, and that the pressure is going to cause problems. He told me he drinks vodka every night to feel happy. He has a seventeen-year-old cat and can't travel because he can't leave his cat alone. He's never been married, has no kids. He still goes on family vacations with his parents even though they are crazy and mean to waiters because he is afraid of upsetting them. "I don't know what I will do when my mother dies," he finally said as I was wrapping up to go. "Have a party?" I asked. His face dropped.

"Oh, no. It's going to be terrible," he said. "She's the one I call when I have problems. I can't imagine her gone."

He limped down the street. He had arthritis in his knee and an underdeveloped calf from surgery he'd had ten years ago. He told me he'd dropped out of three colleges and hadn't finished. For some reason he couldn't explain he doesn't open his mail.

When I got home, I emailed him to say thank you. He wrote back, "It was my pleasure. And thank you for your time. After our meeting it's a no-brainer that I would read a book about adoption. You taught me a lot in little time. I look forward to learning more."

Ten minutes later he wrote, "Btw, is there any relationship between adopted and having a poor sense of direction?"

I couldn't believe it. Just that afternoon, I'd been walking the streets of NYC with absolutely no clue where I was. I thought about this was pretty much always how I felt: drifty, unattached, with no real sense of where I was in the bigger picture. I mean, East Village? East of what? And that it was something I felt embarrassed about, like there was something wrong with me. But when I was out walking, I decided not to care anymore. I decided it was just the way I was. Unmoored.

And his question made me feel less alone in the land of the unmoored wanderers.

ANYTHING BUT THIS

I was in a coffee shop writing about stomach issues. I had interviewed an adopted woman who told me she'd been returned after a few months the first time she was adopted as an infant because of the parents said she too difficult to care for—she had stomach issues.

She told me about how her stomach had always been a problem for her. She took medicine in elementary school, something green, and in sixth grade when she went on her school's week long field trip, her mother had to come get her after three days. "That darn stomach of yours," her mother said on the way home.

The woman now avoids gluten and dairy, but her stomach still is in knots more often than not, a fisted presence in her life that makes relaxing completely impossible.

As I was writing about this I realized I had to go to the bathroom, but it was a small place and there was no toilet. I prayed for mercy and control as I sat in the chair, and I stood up gingerly, but pace was no matter. I could feel my bowels loosen and let go.

Outside the coffee shop, I leaned against some metal railing and felt my bowels release more. It wasn't the best day to have worn pale jeans and no underpants. Luckily, I was in NYC where more than one person had walked the streets with a pantload of shit. I had assumed it wouldn't be me.

I was on 10th and 8th and had a few blocks to go until I was home. I held my large purse behind me like I was a woman so at ease she decided to let her purse hang behind her because she had not a care in the world. My pants felt sticky and dirty and I could not wait to take them off and throw them away.

This was not the first time I'd shit my pants in public. But never, ever, did I think afterwards, *boy, adoption sure does affect me in strange ways.*

My stomach had been a source of discomfort for me almost all my adult life. I was the queen of farting and was used to feeling either bloated or simply uncomfortable in my abdomen. I always blamed it on stress of daily life or leaky gut syndrome or the food I ate or the speed with which I had eaten it. I had never even considered other options.

IT'S COMPLICATED

I don't think I can write about adoption without writing about dating. It would be easier not to, to pretend that my romantic history is the same as anyone's else, to not admit that every single time I go on a new date, my silent plea is, see me, love me, take me home and keep me safe. That, really, I want to get adopted over and over again.

Perhaps you can imagine how well this has gone.

I decided to work on what my therapist labeled "attachment disorder" on Tinder. I was going to date until I didn't try to get adopted. I went on 18 dates in two months in San Jose, but then, when I got to New York City, things went into hyper drive. I had twenty-two dates in the first eleven days. I was going to disorder the disorder.

It felt like I was trying to work my way through a wall of men to the other side where I could finally find stillness. When I slowed down and tried to picture what this stillness would look like in male form, I realized it was a male me, only better. Someone unapologetically himself. Someone confident, successful, sexy. I thought about how I cried to my hippie boyfriend about feeling abandoned, and I thought *I am not her*. I thought about how I let myself wear ragged shirts because I wasn't worth more, how I let walk around with a strange hair color because, who was I to complain to my hairdresser?

I would not want to date that guy.

I thought of a quote my yoga teacher often read to us by Marianne Williamson: *Our deepest fear is not that we are inadequate. Our deepest fear is that we are powerful beyond measure. It is our light, not our darkness that most frightens us. We ask ourselves, Who am I to be brilliant, gorgeous, talented, and fabulous? Actually, who are you not to be? You are a child of God. Your playing small does not serve the world. There is nothing enlightened about shrinking so that other people will not feel insecure around you. We are all meant to shine, as children do. We were born to make manifest the glory of God that is within us. It is not just in some of us; it is in everyone and as we let our own light shine, we unconsciously give others permission to do the same. As we are liberated from our own fear, our presence automatically liberates others.*

I realized that in the past I'd chosen men who came with excuses, addictions, strange baggage, because in their failures was room for my own. But what if I wasn't broken? What if I was a strong, creative, loving, successful woman worthy of love and devotion and clarity of mind?

This seemingly very pleasant idea is almost as hard to swallow as a handful of dice. The choking comes when I think about a life with minimal drama, a life filled with acceptance and ease and love. Having these thoughts makes me feel like a porcupine considering a silky robe. My brain, it seems, is hard wired for trauma. One time a boyfriend was hollering about something I had done that was upsetting to him—I'd forgotten to tell the people at the restaurant not to put tomatoes on his pizza—and I looked at him and I thought, *No one else could handle you but me*. I felt a sense of duty, and I stayed with him much longer than was healthy for either of us.

It was like this when I was a kid. I'd see my brothers punch holes through the horsehair plaster walls in our house or I'd watch my mother smack herself and call herself dummy when she made a mistake, and I'd think, *Okay, I must have been brought here for a reason. What can I do to fix everything?*

Could this also be part of adoption? The feeling that you were brought into the family to fix it, that your mother and father had something missing in their lives they hadn't been able to make themselves and they *had rescued you, chosen you*—whatever term people use when they talk about your adoption—and so you learn early on to put your needs second to those around you.

DEAR BETH

I went to the butcher's to get food for dinner. I was talking my head off, excited to be in the city, excited to be in a small kosher deli buying a steak to cook for a man I had recently met online and wanted to impress. The butcher asked me what I was doing in New York when I told him I was from California, and I told him I was writing a book about adoption. "I'm adopted," the tall man behind me said, and I turned around to high-five him.

"What are you writing about?" he asked.

I told him I was writing about my own experience with adoption and my belief that the lives of those adopted and their family members might be easier if adoption was treated like a traumatic event.

"Adoption wasn't traumatic for me," the man said. "My

parents are great. How was it traumatic for you?

"My parents were great too," I said. "But I had some problems. I dropped out of school a bunch of times. I've been married twice. I have trouble holding on to things."

The man nodded. "I dropped out of school a bunch of times, too," he said.

I asked him if I could interview him. He looked at me, thinking. "But you can't use my name," he said. I agreed. I wouldn't use his name. "I wouldn't want my parents to know," he said.

So many adoptees don't even realize the secrecy that is part of their lives. They think it's normal, to have a life that they aren't free to talk about at home. My mother's friend was telling me how much my mother hated to think about my birth mother. She couldn't bear to think about her, is what my mother's friend said. And I knew this as a child, as an adult, and so I talked about my birth mother as little as possible, but my birth mother was part of me, and so denying her was denying myself, and that meant that when my mother said she loved me, I knew she didn't mean she loved all of me. She loved that part she considered hers.

I would have liked the freedom to be myself. What that

means, primarily, is that when I had told my mother that my real mother, the queen, was going to be angry at how I'd been treated when she came back to get me, that my mom had gotten strong instead of weak. I wish that she could have taken me into her arms, even though it would have been like a fisherman trying to grab a caught fish—I would have thrashed and fought against her hold—but it was what I needed. I needed the ordinariness of my life to grab hold of me and show me that it was never going to change. That I was who I was and that was okay. My mother was going to hold on no matter how ugly or disagreeable I got. She wasn't leaving.

I think the next part would have been the hardest. I think I would have benefited from being forced to stay at the dinner table, at camp, at college, at jobs. Even now, I play games with myself. I am usually the first one to leave a party or any kind of social gathering, and so now I make myself stay an hour past the time I first want to leave. I set a timer on my phone.

I am so afraid of not being wanted. I don't think about this consciously, but it's why I tend to leave early. I want, again and again, to leave before I can feel unwanted. But this means I lose the chance, again and again, to make connections with people because just as the party is getting started, I am headed out in the safe bubble of my own company.

If my parents had made me stay, it would have been like putting a furious tiger in a cage with an equally furious tiger. I would have had to fight and face my own fierce heartbreak and anger and confusion.

When a fisherman grabs a fish to pull the hook out, he just holds on until the fish stops struggling. And the fish does stop. It has to. It knows it can't win against the strength of the fisherman's hand. And I think it would have been like that in the kitchen if my mother had held me in my fury. First I would have fought, I might have even said that I hated her and that I wished my real mom would come get me, and then I would have broken down into sobs, crying over the fact that there was no queen in a carriage and that my mother was the mother I had and crying over the fact that I was pushing away the person I loved most in the world, and then, as my mother held me and held me and kissed me and told me she loved me, the real battle would start. *I don't belong here* would siren in my brain along with the twin cries of *You don't know me* and *Soon you will leave* and I would be sick with the need for escape, and this is where my mother would need to hold on for dear life because in my inability to accept acceptance, I would spin like a tornado; I would try to chew off my own arm to escape the hold of her arms because to surrender and to be held would seem like walking through the doors of death. I would cry and shake, cry and shake, and, like a wild animal shaking off the trauma of a near death experience, I would shake off the trauma of abandonment, and I would soften, surrender, and hold on to her like my life depended on it.

IT'S DARK IN HERE

There was only one Tinder date that scared me. We'd spent a day together walking the High Line and then drinking and talking at a bar, and the next night we had our second date. I liked him a lot—he was funny and smart and sweet. He'd bought me a $19 Metro Card when we took the subway to the West Side instead of the $3.50 for a single ride. It meant a lot to me, that he thought of trips I might take past the day we were spending together.

The day of our second date, I told the mustached butcher that I wanted a piece of meat that would make Kevin fall in love with me.

266

He sold me a heavy piece of New York Strip and told me to rub garlic over the surface and salt it before searing it in a cast iron pan and then putting it in the oven for 10 minutes. "Too little time is okay," he said. "You can always cook it more. Too much means you need ketchup."

He came around the counter and demonstrated how to use the webbing between my thumb and forefinger to simulate the feel of rare, medium, and well done. "Let me know what happens," he said. "He'd be crazy not to love you."

I left the store euphoric. I had a home, a man to cook for, a book to write, and a butcher who gave me a discount. Granted, the home wasn't mine, the man was a second date, the book might be nothing in the end but a cataloguing of my thoughts on being adopted, and the butcher might cut five dollars off anyone's bill that was over thirty dollars, but at the time I wasn't thinking like that: I was thinking everything was going to be okay.

Hours later Kevin and I were in bed, our stomachs full of delicious steak, and I looked up at him, at the GI Joe build of his upper body, at his closed eyes, at the strange angle he was lying on top of me, and it was like I slipped from a romantic comedy to a horror movie. There was something wrong. I didn't know what it was, but all the alarms in my body were ringing. His laugh was not real, it was shallow and distracted; he was not looking at me, he was looking past me, thinking of when he would start to tear me apart. I thought about asking him to get up, to get dressed, to get in his car and drive back to New Jersey even though it was past midnight and we'd both been drinking, but I was afraid that would be the spark that would set him off and that he would choke me and rip me to pieces. We'd been making jokes all night about who was stronger, and every time we both agreed that he was. I was strong, but he was a weight lifter. I tried to even out my breathing and not panic. I paid close attention to his hands, and when they came close to my neck or my face I prepared myself to slam my palm into his nose.

I mentally listed what I knew about him. I knew his first name, that he was a lawyer and that he taught philosophy at a college, but I didn't know his last name and the names of the places he worked. I was gob smacked by my stupidity. How had this happened? How had I let a stranger into my place, into my bed? It was going to be the worst death: frightening and ugly and sexual. My daughter. I thought about my daughter. She was so clean and pure and good, and I was going to drag the dirtiness of who I was into her life.

I was no different than the girl in juvenile hall who got herself into prostitution because she was convinced she was worthless. But instead of money, I'd gotten a Metro Card. I saw that it didn't matter how much I tried to change, at the end of the day I was a human being whose mother had cast her aside and there was no fixing the damage that was done. I could act: I could put up my sails and pretend I had self-esteem and self-worth and that I was a real person out in the world, but I was a shell, a fake, and there was nothing anybody could do about it. What kept my stomach in a state of distress was the constant tap-dance of *I'm real I'm real I'm real* and now I'd finally run out of tricks and I was going to get the kind of end I deserved.

I wished I'd had the strength of character to remain at home alone at nights instead of feeling the necessity to be with a man. My lack of self-reliance was going to get me killed. My eyes filled with tears as the man kissed my neck. I kissed him back and prayed for him to be kind.

The next morning we went to get coffee together and laughed all the way to the coffee shop and back. Kevin did everything right: he held the door, he took my arm, he laughed at my jokes, he said interesting things, and yet there was still something dark under the surface that frightened me. I sat on the couch with him and drank my coffee and ate my muffin and I felt my body soften as I looked at his face and I watched him talk and I wondered if this was the beginning of love.

I HEAR YOU

I was going for a bike ride with Kevin. The steak had worked, and if he didn't love me, he seemed to like me a lot. He was a lawyer and protective of how much he told me about himself, but I did know that part of his childhood had been about negotiating with his father's verbal and physical abuse.

We were riding up a hill, and a small group of people was parked at the top while a little girl battled to stop her bike. "Use the brakes, not your feet!" her mother shrieked. The little girl struggled to lift her feet off the ground, but then the bike picked up momentum.

We passed the group and Kevin turned around and said, "Did you hear that mom? She called that girl 'idiot'. She muttered it, but you know that girl heard."

I shook my head. I hadn't heard. You only hear what you are

listening for, perhaps, and my parents had never intentionally said an unkind thing about me, and so I didn't listen for other parents to malign their children. I thought about all the things this man's father must have called him, all the words he had heard that made him feel small or worthless. I thought about his car. He drives a beautiful black Mercedes, shiny with silver trim. The front of the car is immaculate. It looks like it should be in a cigar commercial with the leather seats and softly glowing dashboard. The back of the car looks like it belongs to a sixteen-year-old stoner. There are empty Gatorade bottles, newspaper pages, receipts, food wrappers, coat hangers, sneakers with dangling laces covering the seat and floor.

There are so many ways for parents to abandon their children. So many ways for us to carry these memories into adulthood, to remember our general lack of worth, to give us reason to fuck up the nice things that we have because we know in our guts that we don't deserve them.

And I knew it wasn't going to matter how much I loved him. I was like the parent to an adopted child in this relationship—no matter how fully I embraced and adored who he was, he'd be too busy listening to his past to hear me tell him he was perfect. And in this, I was leaving myself wide opened to feel abandoned and unwanted. I was still so *adopted*.

SQUEEZE ME

Having issues of self-loathing because you were once abandoned is like a donut being disgusted by its own filling. There's nothing the donut can do about its filling—it is what it is. What a waste of a donut.

TEMPER

I had dinner with a woman whose ten-year-old granddaughter was adopted from Vietnam. The woman was telling me about how charming and smart and funny her granddaughter is. "But she's so manipulative," she said. "She flies of the handle with no notice and my son and his wife give in almost every time."

I asked about the adoption process. "My son and his wife went to Vietnam for six weeks," she said. "They went through the whole process. The caretakers at the orphanage were wonderful. Warm.

Caring. The baby was either given up at birth, or," she looked down at her lap, picked at something on her skirt—we'd shared a bottle of wine and she was talking more than usual—and said in a low aside, "we hate to think about it, maybe she'd been sold."

I thought about this child, how she lost her mother, the caretakers at the orphanage, her culture, her country, her continent, and how the love of a woman and a man not related to her by blood was supposed to erase the losses. How could anger not be an issue? How could this child not have a volcano of confusing feelings inside of her?

And, how could she not be charming and manipulative? If you're afraid your life is going to disappear any second, aren't you going to tap dance a little faster to keep the hook from grabbing you? Even if you don't know you have this fear, even if you don't know why you're dancing that fast, even if you are smiling at someone when something inside is telling you to set fire to the world?

"It's complicated," I said.

She looked up at me. "Thinking about it is almost unbearable."

GOOD NIGHT

I dated a man who had also been adopted. When it came time to say goodnight, one time I shut my own head in the car door in our mutual race to get away from each other first. The importance of saying goodbye first was keeping your power.

A FART IS STILL A FART

I read an article in the Huffington Post called *Ten Things Adoptees Want You to Know*, and so I emailed an adopted friend of mine to write his own list. At first he was uncertain and only sending a few at a time, but soon he was on a roll—"Hey!" he wrote at one point. "I'm having fun!"— and I could not stop laughing, kept writing hahahaha in response to each message, and then Number 11 popped up and I stopped laughing.

1. Don't try to pretend I look like you.

2. Don't freak out when I do things no one in the history of your family ever did.

3. I probably am really messed up - please don't think I'm crazy.

4. Return me within 30 days if you have any doubts.

5. Read up on "abandonment" issues.

6. If you can have your own baby, please please please return me now.

7. If you can't have a baby, maybe it was God's way.

8. Hey, did you try a puppy first?

9. Hey, thanks for telling me I was adopted now I feel even more outcast than ever.

10. I will initially say I'm fine with you being my parents but over time I will wonder if that is true. I will then attempt to find my real parents which will cause you great pain. When I find them, I will probably hate both pairs.

11. IMPORTANT: When I am beaten up by the bully on the corner, don't fuckin' back away saying you don't know what to do. Defend me like you would defend the kid that came out of your own uterus.

12. I will be deeply empathetic.

As I read his list, I heard my friend's laughing voice. It reminded me of when I was a kid in school and my friends and I thought to look up the word "fart" in the class dictionary. My guess was that my friend took a childlike pleasure in saying the things he'd felt most of his life but also felt were, for various reasons, wrong to say, and was and was talking gleeful pleasure in slipping under the doorway of propriety.

But, at the end of the day, a fart is still a fart, and a person's angry thoughts about adoption can still exist, even though most people try to hold them in and so to the rest of the world they seem non-existent or inconsequential.

WHAT CAN I DO?

I talked with a man who had a son with drug problems. He'd adopted his son and thought there had to be something in the DNA that made his son turn to narcotics because it was nothing that he and his wife or anyone in their families had ever done.

He said that the boy hated his birth parents for giving him up when he was younger, but that when he was thirty, he started to search for his birth mother and ended up receiving a loving letter from her with a photograph to which the son has yet to respond.

If you grow up hating your birth parents, how do you not hate at least a little part of yourself? Why wouldn't you turn to drugs just to take the edge of these feelings? Being hated by someone else is hard enough, being hated by yourself is exhausting. If my body liked drugs, I probably would have been an addict too. Instead, I chose to numb out on brownie batter and Peanut M&M's and Diet Coke. Eat and drink enough of that stuff and you can feel out of your body and mind in no time.

I asked the father if the son would be willing to talk to me about adoption some time. The man shook his head. He didn't even have to think about it. "He won't talk to anybody about it," he said.

"But you don't think his drug problems have anything to do with his feelings about being adopted?" I asked.

"We told him he was adopted from the get go. It was never a secret or something to be ashamed about in our house."

"You said that when he was eighteen he was allowed to search for his birth parents."

"Yes. That is the state law."

"And so before he was eighteen it was illegal for him to search."

"I'm not sure illegal is the right word. It's just how it is. The records are sealed, but at eighteen the child can file a request to be put in contact with either of the birth parents if either also puts in a request."

"Put in a request to meet your roots. That sounds so funny. It's like pouring concrete around the base of a tree and telling it not to look down until it's an adult. The poor tree would probably be either terrified or ashamed of what was down there—whatever, unknown, awful thing had to be kept hidden from it for so long."

The man took a long breath. "I love my son," he said.

"I know you do," I said. "I bet he loves you, too."

BLINK

A woman who was adopted wrote this to me: *My birth mother says she never looked at me, but I know that's a lie. I looked at her. She was my mother for an hour. If you are anywhere for an hour, you look around. An hour is a long time, considering love can happen between traffic lights.*

KITE

I thought about standing in front of the computer and trying to write about my mother. I thought about how what I wanted was to merge into the memory of her, one I created. What I wanted was to go back to the early 70's when I was a child, when Richard Nixon, Indira Gandhi, Elvis, Bobby Fisher, and Vietnam were in the news and gas was about 55 cents a gallon. When mothers went to the beach for summer vacations and fathers arrived Fridays after work with their neckties loosened and a sweating beer quick in hand. Sunburns were not seen as a health threat and we could hitchhike to the wharf with our fishing rods whenever we wanted to earn candy money by catching squid we could sell to the fish store as bait.

I wanted to sit in the long dry grass in the field behind the barn, the place we would go to fly kites, but this time I wanted it to be me and my mom, and I wanted my mother to sit in the grass and for me to sit on her lap, cradled in her arms, rocked like a baby. I wanted her to smell my hair, to breathe me in, and I wanted the two of us to cry about the fact that I was adopted. I wanted us to cry because she wasn't my biological mother even though it felt she was. I wanted us to cry for the fact that I had a birth mother out there whom I didn't know. I wanted us to grieve my adoption together so that then we could love each other with whole hearts.

ONE TO YALE ONE TO JAIL

"I have two sons in their forties," the man said. "One is natural born and the other is adopted. When I was in court defending my adopted son, I said. 'I have one in Yale, one in jail,' and the judge laughed. "He's been sober now for 16 years, got a good job, but he's always been messed up. I get that you are talking to me because he's is adopted, but I have to tell you I think his problems happened because his birth parents must have been addicts. He's always said that being adoption is not a problem for him. In fact, he almost never talks about it. He searched for his birth mother once, but he gave up almost immediately."

An hour later he called back. His son had told him I could call the next day if I wanted to ask him questions.

The next day I called the son and he didn't answer. This happened a number of times. My guess is that if adoption hadn't been a problem, he wouldn't have started the search or ended it so abruptly. He wouldn't have volunteered to talk to me and then changed his mind.

THE MIRACLE

If I hadn't been adopted, I wouldn't know any of the people I know. I wouldn't have had my parents, my grandparents, my aunts, my uncles, my cousins. My Uncle Roger. Maybe I wouldn't have had a mother who was a writer, a mother who made me love writing, whose dream to write a book was also my dream. I wouldn't have any of my memories. I wouldn't remember being a little girl on Martha's Vineyard. I wouldn't remember the day Sam came to us as a wild-haired two-year old. I wouldn't remember running the streets of my town as a sixteen-year-old with David Callaghan after midnight. I can hardly breathe as I type these things. I wouldn't have had my pets: Lily, Jet, Polly, Mona, Katie, and all the others: the gerbils, the rat, the birds, the turtles, the fish, the rabbit, the guinea pigs, the other cats, the other dogs. I wouldn't have the love my parents had poured my way, their adoration, their care. I wouldn't remember the smell of our house, their clothes.

Most unthinkable, I wouldn't have had my daughter. Keats wouldn't even *exist.*

MAYBE IT'S THAT GUY

My half-sister told me she thought Daniel was my father. This was shocking to me because Daniel was the patriarch of the family my birth mother had stayed with in Michigan while she was pregnant. Daniel was the local minister, and he had written many young adult books. He had got in touch with me when he heard that I had contacted my half-siblings, and, until a year or two ago, he had made a sustained effort to keep in touch with me. I was afraid he had died and didn't want to ask or know. I had five or six long handwritten letters from him that talked of simple things, what he had his wife had been doing, small bits of family history. His handwriting was gorgeous, like a textbook on cursive, and he used sheet after sheet of yellow lined paper. He once sent me a photograph of his wife and him sitting behind my pregnant birth mother at the beach. All of them were smiling and the wind was lightly blowing their hair back. My birth mother was easy in her bathing suit, lounging back, apparently not caring at all that she was a little chubby with child. They all looked so happy.

I had tracked a friend of my birth mother's down, and she had told me, via email, that she really didn't have much to share, but she suspected that my birth father was my birth mother's boyfriend, Fred, and that she didn't remember Fred's last name. She remembered that Fred had played organ at the church, but that my search was over because she was fairly sure Fred was dead.

My birth mother, of course, had told me that my father had been a tall, healthy young man from the Coast Guard. So there was that guy. And there was the fact that my birth mother had lied to me repeatedly. It felt impossible to know what was true about my origins. Any day someone could come around and tell me a new story and there I would be with a new father.

DIAMONDS

My friend was talking about the fact that she was adopted. She talked for an hour about the pain she carried, about feeling misunderstood, about self-hatred. She talked for another hour about fearing abandonment from almost everyone; she talked about keeping her circle of friends small so there was less chance of being left. She talked about the fact that her husband would never know her. She told me she'd never talked to an adopted person about adoption. She said she couldn't remember feeling this comfortable talking with another person.

And then she took a deep breath and looked around. She touched her heart and she smiled. "You can't ever get inside of it," she said, and I was unclear whether she was talking about her heart or adoption, but I wasn't about to speak. Her face was shining. She lay her hand flat on her chest, like a mother would to soothe a child.

She looked me in the eye. She stopped smiling and took another long breath and the hardness I had gotten used to in her face softened. "My adoption is something I have that no one can take away," she finally said. "It makes me mysterious to people. They see me and they say *There's something about her I'll never understand.*

She tapped herself on the chest and looked up to the ceiling. "I love that," she said. "I'm a mystery."

I looked at her and realized that, while there is so much sadness that is part of being adopted, she and I had been given everything; we were smart, loving, funny, capable, strong, and we had people in our lives who loved us. We didn't have to believe that any of that was true, but if we DID then our lives had a much better chance of being spectacular. We could either choose to suffer at a certain point or we could say fuck it and throw off the burden and shine.

OH

"When are you coming home?" Antonia asked as soon as I picked up the phone.

I shrugged, but she couldn't see because she was in California and I was in New York.

I was sitting on the white leather couch where the fabulously famous author had written her best seller.

"You have a home here, you know," Antonia said. "You can stay at my place as long as you need. It would help me out. You can chip in when you can."

"Thank you. Maybe in a few weeks."

"Keats was here to get your car."

"Yeah, she told me."

"Holy shit."

"I know."

"I mean, you showed me pictures, but I was shocked. She's so beautiful. So grown up. And she looks like you so much now. I couldn't stop staring. She used to look more like her dad, but now it's like your face with Asian features."

I held my breath. I didn't want her to stop talking.

"Do you know what she said to me?"

"No."

"She said, 'I am my mother's daughter, after all,' when we talked about her decision to major in Art History instead of Environmental Science. She loves you so much. She told me that the trip you guys took to Italy was the best trip of her life. She told me that she misses you and that she wants you to come home."

Tears streamed down my face. I hadn't failed.

AND THEN WHAT?

I went upstairs, took the sheets off the bed, put them in the washing machine, and went into the bathroom to shower. Afterwards, I got my phone and lay on the living room phone and deleted my Tinder account.

Good bye Dan Whom I Called Whit, Black Glenn, White Glenn, Andy Who Loved All Women, Funny Tony, Travelling Guy, French Guy, Artist Mark, Chiro Ken, Irish Guy Who Left His Family Back In Ireland, Guy Whose Profile Picture Was Twenty Years Old, Guy Who Was Voting for Trump, Drunk Guy, Old Comic, Pencil Guy, Beautiful Peter With The Tracks, Walking Travelogue Belgium Dude, Sweet Hippie Short Guy, Tall Dude Who Worked With Diane Sawyer, and good bye to all that texting to the men I never even met. "How are you today?" "What are you doing" "Come live with me. I have an extra room."

I lay on the floor and thought about Woody Allen. I thought about how beautiful the world was in black and white. I thought about the scene in *Manhattan* where Woody Allen and Diane Keaton talk in shadow against the pitted planet and I closed my eyes and almost fell asleep.

An hour later, I got a text: *What are you doing?* he asked. *I am lying on the floor*, I wrote. *Do you need soup? he asked. Toast? Bananas? Chamomile tea? Honey?* I thought about it, about this man who didn't kill me taking time from work, driving from New Jersey to New York just to bring me a bag full of groceries I could easily go get myself. I didn't know if he had ten Tinder dates lined up for the upcoming month. I didn't know if he even really liked me or if I was just a way to cut the pain of the world. I was leaving in a few weeks. He had made up an extra bed in his house in case I wanted to sleep alone. We were so alike. You can dance with your mirror image, but you can't hold it close.

As I waited for him to arrive, I sat up and got back to writing this book and cried my way through a chapter on how much I loved my mother. I had no idea what would happen next, no idea where I'd live, how I'd support myself, and I saw that I had to work on envisioning my dreams of the future. It was easy to imagine disaster; joy was murky.

I wanted my book to be a success. I wanted to go out into the world as the spokesperson for the adopted person and to help others find relief in recognition; I wanted my daughter to have a rewarding and fulfilling life; I wanted to be financially independent; I wanted to be able to live the way I was living now in New York, free to follow my impulses, surrounded by friends and vitality and art. But most of all, I wanted love.

But it wasn't about the love I could get, I realized: It was about the love I could give. I'd had love all my life, and it never seemed like enough or the right kind. To wait for love, to dance for love, to sing for love: all were like painting in the rain. I wanted something real. I wanted *to* love.

My phone dinged. "*Mama*," the message from Keats read. "*I want to come visit you in NYC after finals. I just have to schedule it between field hockey practices. Can you get me a ticket?*"

Yes.

My daughter was coming to see me. I hadn't lost her by leaving.

A MEDITATION FOR ADOPTED PEOPLE

These are the soles of my feet. These are my toes. There are the tops of my foot. These are my ankles. These are my calves. These are my shins. There are my kneecaps. There are the backs of my knees. These are the fronts of my thighs. These are the backs of my thighs. This is my pelvis. The is my butt. This is my back, my spine. This is my stomach, my guts, all my internal organs, my heart, my lungs. This is my throat. These are my shoulders. This is the outside of my upper arms. This is the outside of my forearms. These are the backs of my hands. These are my palms. These are my fingers. These are my thumbs. This is the inside of my forearms. This is the inside of my upper arms. These are my armpits. This is the back of my neck. This is the front of my neck. This is my face. These are my ears. This is my scalp.

Be here. It is okay to be here.

MY PEEPS

I liked living in Los Angeles when I was in my twenties because I never knew what I would see next. People pushing each other across the street on hospital beds; people doing their grocery shopping in curlers and pajamas. Doing lines at a red light in their

Porsches. The pulsing energy in Los Angeles is *are you famous?* and *are you beautiful?* Every person is quickly evaluated and either a cause for excitement or dismissal. It was like living on a movie set. It was fun and exhausting and sad.

Growing up outside of Boston had been like going to fourth grade. It was solid and safe and the trick was not to dream too big. Just do what your neighbors did and everything would be fine. Think that you were *wicked smaht* and that the rest of the world were *fuckin' retahds*.

I moved to Northern California to live in the area where my husband had grown up, to be married and have a baby and to raise that child in that hilly, green place that is like an SUV commercial. There is something sweet about living in a place where everyone wears the same clothes, has the same color hair, and goes to the same gym. The line at the car wash is always long and the coffee shops are crowded.

I loved the feeling of being *other* when I was in California— palm trees were still a novelty to me after twenty years. The lack of real weather: blue sky, blue sky, blue sky. My California friends expected it, but every day that I woke up part of me thought *are you kidding me?* and I felt a pressure to be outside: to hike, to swim, to run, because it was a sunny day, and when I grew up, a sunny day was something to celebrate whereas on the East Coast, the grey days made sitting inside easier, an invitation to hibernate and still. But after a while *other* gets tiring. How long can you live outside the bubble before you yearn for *in*?

When I got to New York City to write this book, I was home in a way I never was in the other places. It made me wonder if the place where you are conceived and born is part of who you are, part of your roots.

23 AND ME

A friend suggested I do DNA testing, and so I went on the 23 and Me website and watched a video about an adopted person finding family members, and through tears I pulled out my credit card and filled out the order form.

It was going to take six to eight weeks to get the results once I got the test tube and returned my saliva sample, so I figured by midsummer I might have more information about my genetic history.

I didn't have many expectations. I was curious to see what part of the world most of my relatives had come from.

A few weeks later, when my daughter was with me in New York, I got an email saying my results were ready. We sat on the bed together and scrolled through the pages, laughing at some of the information we were getting: people with my genes were not likely to have a cleft chin, curly hair, or dimples. Since neither of us had any of these, I was wondering if I'd thrown away $199 for useless facts.

There was a Carrier Status page, and that one made me nervous, for it listed 36 rare genetic disorders that might be present in my DNA. Each category had a brief description and then with a "variant not detected" or "variant detected" at the end. I held my breath and quickly scrolled through all 36, reading only the variant status.

When we saw that all were cleared, we went back through and laughed at the strangeness of some of the disorders. "Maple Syrup Urine Disease Type 1B" had me convinced that this whole thing was a waste of time.

And then we opened DNA relatives, and at the very top of the list was a man's name with "uncle" next to it. We shared 29.1 of the same DNA. His last name was not the same as my birth mother's last name. "I bet that's your birth father's brother," Keats said, and I just stared at the name, unable to comprehend the information.

There was a box where I could write a message to my new uncle, so I wrote that I was adopted and looking for relatives. I left my email address and phone number. I went on Facebook, typed in his name, and his profile and picture came up. He looked like my dad. He also—his cheekbones, his teeth, his gaze—looked like me.

INFORMATION

Two days later I got a phone call. And the most amazing thing happened. I talked with the brother of my birth father. Jessie, my new uncle, said that he did have a tall, blonde brother, Jacob, who had been twenty-one and in the Coast Guard in 1964.

I found a pen and a piece of paper and wrote JACOB on the top. I wrote "successful" and "professor" and "married" and "no children". I wrote "very private". I wrote "sober".

I could feel the roots sink and the trunk of myself get stronger.

Jessie told me he would contact Jacob and try to convince him to at least talk to me, but that he was a very private person and happily married and so the chances were slim. I wrote "no".

There was going to be another parent to refuse contact with me. I felt so tired. It was good enough to know he existed. To know who he was and that he was smart and athletic and, according to his brother, a good person. I already had a father. Now I know the name of my birth father. I wanted a photograph, but I didn't want to make Jesse uncomfortable by asking, so after our call I went online and remarkably enough, found nothing. My birth father had published a number of text books, and so the Amazon links to those were online, but somehow he had managed to keep the rest of himself out of the internet spotlight.

THE INSIDE

My brain sounded like this: I found my birth father. I found my birth father. I found my birth father. I found my birth father. I found my birth father. I found my birth father. I found my birth father. I found my birth father. I found my birth father. I found my birth father. I found my birth father. I found my birth father. I found my birth father. I found my birth father. I found my birth father. I found my birth father.

I felt more grounded. Taller. Stronger. But I also felt bereft. The loss was still there.

A ROOM OF ONE'S OWN

Before I left New York, a had a small dinner party. I invited a woman I'd met at the Montana writer's retreat, a woman I'd met at the Martha's Vineyard writer's retreat along with her husband, a writer twice nominated for the Pulitzer; a Pulitzer-prize winning photographer I'd met on Tinder and had become friends with, and, best of all, my daughter was there.

We were gathered in the home I'd been staying. My friend's husband told me I was a vagrant with discerning taste after he saw the apartment that could have easily been in *Architectural Dig*est or *People Magazine*. There were enormous chandeliers, couches made of velvet, soft rugs underfoot. There was luxury everywhere, and I'd lived there for two and a half months because a writer knew what another writer needed most: space and time to write.

I looked around the table at the group of beautiful, smart people laughing and arguing and sharing stories. Where adoption used to be a handicap, something that kept me quiet, it was now a springboard to my life. I had owned its importance and its impact and now I felt free. I could talk about adoption all I wanted. But it no longer felt like a burden or a weight in my gut. It was like talking about my hair or the length of my arms. It was just part of me.

I had spider webbed things I loved: my daughter was there, my new friends, and we were talking about writing, living in the city, photography, my daughter's major in school.

I felt connected. I felt real. I was so happy.

Just months earlier, I'd been isolating myself in California, huddled into the sadness and frustration of not knowing how to live a life that felt real. So many people had helped me on this Write or Die Journey. I'd been given a place to live, money, food, emotional support, stories, and love. As important as it was for me to tell my story, it was equally important, as an adopted person seeking peace in herself and in the world, to see the value of connection. To see the beauty of the web and of my place in it. I still hurt, but the love inside me was bigger.

NUMBERS

A mother who adopted her son told me this story: *When my son, Ian, was five, and I was explaining how some families did not have open adoptions because the adoptive families were afraid that the birthmother could take some of the child's love from them, he said, "Love is the number 4, not the number 3." I thought, "Too much Sesame Street," and asked him what he meant. He said, "When you give to one, you don't have to take away from another. You can just make more love."*

THE CRACK LETS IN THE LIGHT

I saw a picture of a beautiful Japanese bowl that had what looked like a lightning bolt of gold running down its side. I researched it and found that *kintsugi* is the art of repairing broken pottery with a lacquer mixed with gold, silver, or platinum. The idea is for the beholder to see the damage as part of the history of the thing instead of something to hide or mask.

CAN YOU GO ANY FASTER?

When Keats went back to California, I left New York and went to New Jersey for the last four days of Write or Die. I stayed with Kevin and worked during the days while he was at his office.

At night we'd go downstairs to the restaurant and eat and drink Manhattans and then go back upstairs and watch a video or play Guitar Hero. We got high every night. I thought I hated pot, but much to my surprise, I liked how I felt when I smoked with him. I'd always had the sense that in the life that was really mine I lived in a trailer and was a bartender and had a boyfriend who had a motorcycle. I thought in the life that was really mine I smoked and drank, and so when I would lie around with Kevin and take drags from the metal one-hitter that got almost too hot to hold the more we smoked, I felt I was home.

He wasn't like the other men. He was a storyteller and jumped from New Jersey street banter to Greek myths to tales of his Jewish aunts. Listening to him made me feel like a little kid: hungry to learn, hungry to hear more. He didn't grope me; he barely paid my body much attention except to praise it, tell me I was strong, search my arms and legs with his hands for muscle. He loved Crossfit and challenged himself almost daily to surpass whatever he had done the day or week before. Until my mother died, I had done yoga, swam laps in the pool, rode my bike up steep Los Gatos hills, but when my mother disappeared, so did my strength. Soon the best I could do was walk, and I walked for hours. Forward motion was good, but if I challenged myself in any way, tried to run, tried to stretch, tried to move out of the robot movement of one foot in front of the other, my muscles would burn and quickly fail, and I'd start to cry.

"Look at how strong you are," Kevin would say he watched me walk across the room. "You are amazing."

To have someone who looked like he could lift a building tell me I was strong *made* me strong. It made me want to do push-ups, ride my bike, go for a swim. When he was at work I streamed yoga classes online and did the vinyasas, did the balancing posas, went upside down. I made my body burn and shake, but this time I didn't cry; this time I breathed through the pain and started feeling better.

One night he took me to dinner with his best friend and his best friend's wife, and it felt like we'd been doing this as a couple

300

forever, hanging out, eating, laughing. I loved his friend, loved his friend's wife, and I saw how much they adored Kevin, and it made me like him even more. I knew he was trying. His best friend told me I was just the second woman Kevin had introduced them to in seven years, and I could see that his friends liked me and that they were excited Kevin had met someone who was clearly a good match for him. But he could barely stand to touch me, and when I told him how much I liked him, sometimes he would say he liked me too, and sometimes he would say, "I'm so fucked up. You should pick someone else."

It was strange to meet someone wonderful and to know that he was so lost in his own pain of hating himself that he couldn't let himself love me. I wondered if that was how it had been for both my husbands.

In the car on the way home from dinner, I looked at Kevin from across the distance of our lives and wished he could see himself the way I did. Wished he could see he was perfect. I told him that, and he said he looked at me the same way, harbored the same wish for me. Later that night he said, "Maybe I'll tie you up some time." I asked if that was something he had done before. He shrugged and smiled. "Maybe." I asked him what he would do after he tied me up, and he looked off to the side and shrugged again. "I don't know. Maybe go into the kitchen and get something to eat." I laughed and told him that we might have more fun playing Guitar Hero. He nodded. It was so fun to try to get the audience to love you.

On Saturday, we went for a ride on his motorcycle. He pulled out a heavy leather jacket that would have been the height of cool when he got it in the 1980's and I pulled it on. It was big on me and the sleeves were long and I held on the to the edges of the cuffs with my fingers and felt like a teenager.

As we went ripping down the highway, I thought about letting go. I imagined myself flying off the back of the bike so I could never disappoint another person, never feel I wasn't good enough. Living as yourself is hard when you think you are supposed to be someone else.

I shifted forward and held on a little more tightly. He was wearing a black motorcycle jacket thick with padding, and so it didn't matter how hard I held on, all I felt was jacket.

When I left his place early the next morning to catch my flight, I didn't look back. Next time, I would choose someone who had learned to love himself enough so that he was able to love me.

302

Someone who didn't have to get high every night. Someone who wouldn't let me walk out the door.

HERE

Planes were slow to take off from LaGuardia, and my plane sat on the tarmac for almost an hour. I listened to Zola Jesus on my headphones and cried. Goodbye beautiful apartment; goodbye Annie and Sam at Third Rail Coffee; goodbye guy with the gold teeth at Westside Market who made my salad every day; goodbye dirty subway; goodbye Strand Bookstore; goodbye ten thousand restaurants and bars and theaters; goodbye beautiful, wild masses of people living their lives right there on the street: arguing, yelling, kissing, fighting for space. Goodbye Write or Die. I'd had a room of my own for 93 days. I'd done it. My mother had died before she finished her book, but I lived to finish mine.

I flew to Chicago where I had a layover before my connecting flight to San Jose. I was dry-eyed now, happy with travel, excited about the next day when I'd get to see Keats. I looked at my phone as I walked through O'Hare and saw an email from a man I'd interviewed about his adopted son. The man had seen my Facebook post about finding my birth father and had volunteered to do some research for me. The heading to his email was "birth father" and there, in the body of the text, was a blurry photograph of a man. I could barely make out his features, but I couldn't stop staring at it. I bumped into a pilot who was carrying an iced coffee. "It's helpful to look up when you walk," he said.

I showed him my phone. "This is my birth father," I said. "I've never seen him before. What do you think?"

The pilot took my phone and looked at the picture. "He looks like a Republican."

We laughed. "He looks like a good guy," the pilot said. "This is a huge day for you."

"This day is a miracle," I said.

I took my phone back from the pilot and went to sit at the bar where I proceeded to show the picture to the woman sitting next to me. We talked about fathers and husbands and the day a pregnant woman had showed up at her door asking to speak to her husband. "My first husband," the woman said. "That day was a game changer."

Having sex is so complicated. Sometimes people get left behind.

TA DA

Two weeks later my birth father sent me an email and the tag line was "your search is over". His brother had told him about me and what I had said of the rape, and my birth father assured me that I had been "conceived in passion, not rape". He gave me the link to a video he was in on Youtube, but, no matter how many times I watched it, I didn't feel anything. I looked for myself in his face, but I didn't see it; maybe a little around the eyes and in the shape of the ears. Looking at him was like eating the wafer cookies my grandmother used to serve that didn't taste like anything no matter how long I left them in my mouth.

I was back in *The Wizard of Oz,* but now Toto had pulled the curtain and the wizard was just a man. I wanted a white horse. I wanted a hero. I wanted a genie who would sprinkle me with magic dust that made me feel I had the right to be in the world. I wasn't searching for someone who looked like he could stand in line at

Target for fifteen minutes without complaining. He looked like a dad, but I already had a dad.

I felt the opposite of curious. If my birth father had called and asked me to dinner that night, I would have to think about it. There was so much potential for rejection. I got my yoga mat out and lay on it and cried. My life was my life—there wasn't some other magical reality on the other side. I felt like the inside of a flower, or the very center of a bruise.

The whole journey wasn't what I expected. I thought I would come back from doing Write or Die somehow taller or shinier or magically rich, but I came back myself and, truth be told, angry. What used to manifest itself as depression and confusion had changed to fury. I was angry that I was in debt, angry that I didn't have a job. I was angry that I hadn't held myself in greater esteem all my life. I was angry at the waste of it.

I was angry, but I was also proud. I'd finally done the thing I'd been trying to do for thirty years, and that felt amazing.

So there was the question of what to do with my life. I had cleared the slate and now I had to figure out what the Anne who had told her story wanted to do next.

WE ASK QUESTIONS

The first person I wrote to when I heard from my birth father was HBL. I wanted to tell him that I was excited. I wanted to tell him that hearing from my birth father made me love my own father even more. He wrote back almost immediately. *Yesterday when my son and I were together, we were walking between holes on the disc golf course and I looked at his back and wondered what was inside of him. I wondered, as you've had your first communication with your birth father, what his mind thinks or will think about his birth father. I wondered if he has the same feelings you did, you do. I wonder if he feels abandonment. I wonder if inside of him is a cauldron of emotion related to his adoption.*

I wonder all of these things but on some level I'm afraid to know. It's easier to pretend none of it exists, but I know better now.

HBL was right: it's so much easier to pretend the trauma of adoption doesn't exist. But I know better now.

It was an amazing experience to have a famous author give me her apartment for almost three months because she believed in my writing, to tell people I was a writer when I was living in New York, to have the time and space to listen to myself for three months, to pay attention to my story and to finally get it down on paper. To make new friends. To fall in love with a city and the sound of my own voice.

"Where have you been?" one of my yoga teachers asked when I was back in California. I told her I'd been in New York to write a book about being adopted. She took my arm. "I'm adopted, too," she said, and she had that look that I'd come to know. It was a look that said, *I can't wait to talk to you because you are going to understand me.*

SUNSHINE

My daughter texted to ask if I could have lunch with her and her boyfriend. She'd never asked this before, and I wondered if she was pregnant or if they were going to tell me they were engaged. I'd seen her a week earlier after I'd gotten home from New York, but she'd been busy with friends since then.

I waited for them in the restaurant, and they blew in, these two tall, lean teenagers who already were brown from the summer. "We just wanted to hang out with you," Keats said as we hugged hello. "It's been too long."

It was all I could do to sit across the table from them and not burst into tears. They were so beautiful. The day before I had met a man at a coffee shop who, when he heard I'd written about adoption, had said, "We are born physically alive but spiritually dead. It's not until we accept God as the Father that we find our spirit. We are all adopted children of God." His eyes were gentle and even if I didn't believe in God, I liked the idea that we are all adopted in love and that it is the acceptance of this love that brings us our spirit.

Right before Thelma and Louise drive off the cliff, Thelma turns to Louise and says, "Let's do it. Let's keep going." Louise says, "Are you sure?" and Thelma nods. They kiss, the light and the wind wild in their hair, and then Thelma guns the car and off they fly into the dusty blue. That's one way to end a story, but when I looked at my daughter, I wanted another way.

Louise had shot Thelma's attacker, and I'd gone rogue and told my story. I'd given it to my father and he'd read it, killing any illusion that Pretty Perfect Princess Anne existed. There was no more hiding for me and it was a raw feeling. I felt exposed and ashamed for having needs, for having made a mess of many things, for not having been the perfect child that my parents might have hoped for when they signed the papers making me theirs.

I also felt free.

THE END

Thank you.

Please forgive me.

I forgive you.

I love you.